ECONOMIC ISSUES, PROBLEMS AND PERSPECTIVES

FEDERAL DEFICIT REDUCTION

CHOICES AND CONSIDERATIONS

ECONOMIC ISSUES, PROBLEMS AND PERSPECTIVES

Additional books in this series can be found on Nova's website under the Series tab.

Additional E-books in this series can be found on Nova's website under the E-book tab.

ECONOMIC ISSUES, PROBLEMS AND PERSPECTIVES

FEDERAL DEFICIT REDUCTION

CHOICES AND CONSIDERATIONS

CARL FRANKEL
AND
DAN IGLEHART
EDITORS

nova publishers
New York

For permission to use material from this book please contact us:
Telephone 631-231-7269; Fax 631-231-8175
Web Site: http://www.novapublishers.com

Additional color graphics may be available in the e-book version of this book.

Library of Congress Cataloging-in-Publication Data

ISBN: 978-1-62417-779-8

Published by Nova Science Publishers, Inc. † New York

CONTENTS

PREFACE

The United States is facing fundamental budgetary challenges. Federal debt held by the public exceeds 70 percent of the nation's annual output or GDP, a percentage not seen since 1950, and a continuation of current policies would boost the debt further. Although debt would decline to 58 percent of GDP in 2022 under the current-law assumptions that underlie the CBO's baseline projections, those projections depend heavily on significant increases in taxes and decreases in spending that are scheduled to take effect at the beginning of January. If, instead, lawmakers maintained current policies by preventing most of those changes from occurring, what the CBO refers to as the alternative fiscal scenario, debt held by the public would increase to 90 percent of GDP 10 years from now and continue to rise rapidly thereafter. This book reviews the scale and sources of the federal government's budgetary imbalance, various options for bringing spending and taxes into closer alignment, and criteria that lawmakers and the public might use to evaluate different approaches to deficit reduction.

Chapter 1 – The United States is facing fundamental budgetary challenges. Federal debt held by the public exceeds 70 percent of the nation’s annual output (gross domestic product, or GDP)—a percentage not seen since 1950— and a continuation of current policies would boost the debt further. Although debt would decline to 58 percent of GDP in 2022 under the current-law assumptions that underlie the Congressional Budget Office’s (CBO’s) baseline projections, those projections depend heavily on significant increases in taxes and decreases in spending that are scheduled to take effect at the beginning of January. If, instead, lawmakers maintained current policies by preventing most of those changes from occurring—what CBO refers to as the alternative fiscal scenario—debt held by the public would increase to 90 percent of GDP 10 years from now and continue to rise rapidly thereafter.

Federal debt cannot grow faster than the nation's output indefinitely, and prolonged increases in debt relative to GDP can cause significant long-term damage to both the government's finances and the broader economy. Higher debt leads to larger federal interest payments; making those payments would eventually require some combination of lower government spending and higher taxes. In addition, increases in debt tend to reduce national saving, leading to more borrowing from abroad and less domestic investment, which in turn reduces the growth of income. Moreover, when debt rises, lawmakers are less able to use tax and spending policies to respond to unexpected challenges, such as economic downturns, natural disasters, or financial crises. Rising debt could itself precipitate a fiscal crisis by undermining investors' confidence in the government's ability to manage the budget, thus making it harder for the government to borrow money at affordable interest rates.

With the population aging and health care costs per person likely to keep growing faster than the economy, the United States cannot sustain the federal spending programs that are now in place with the federal taxes (as a share of GDP) that it has been accustomed to paying. To put the budget on a path that is more likely to be sustainable than if current policies were continued, lawmakers will need to adopt a combination of policies that require people to pay more for their government, accept less in government benefits and services, or both. However, making policy changes that are large enough to shrink the debt relative to the size of the economy—or even to keep the debt from growing—will be a formidable task.

This report reviews the scale and sources of the federal government's budgetary imbalance, various options for bringing spending and taxes into closer alignment, and criteria that lawmakers and the public might use to evaluate different approaches to deficit reduction. The report focuses on CBO's alternative fiscal scenario, rather than on the current-law baseline, to show the size of the policy changes—relative to policies now in place—that would be necessary to put the budget on a more sustainable path.

The discussion builds on estimates that CBO has published previously and, for simplicity, focuses on potential deficit reduction in one year: 2020. Lawmakers could set various deficit reduction goals for that year, such as the following:

- Bringing the federal budget into balance by 2020, which would require policy changes that would reduce the deficit in that year by about $1 trillion relative to the effects of the current policies embodied in CBO's alternative fiscal scenario;

- Keeping debt held by the public the same size relative to GDP at the end of 2020 that it will be early in 2013—roughly 75 percent—which would require deficit reduction of about $500 billion in 2020 compared with the alternative fiscal scenario; or
- Reducing the deficit in 2020 by $750 billion relative to the alternative fiscal scenario, which is roughly the difference between the deficits (excluding interest costs) projected for 2020 in that scenario and in the current-law baseline.

Very few policy changes, taken individually, can shrink the deficit enough to achieve any of those objectives. Ultimately, significant deficit reduction is likely to require a combination of policies, many of which may stand in stark contrast to policies now in place. This report briefly reviews some potential policy changes that lawmakers might consider, showing how far those changes would go toward reducing the deficit in 2020.

The policy options come from CBO's March 2011 report *Reducing the Deficit: Spending and Revenue Options* and from other CBO analyses. They are meant to be illustrative only; many other possible policy changes could be considered.

In evaluating policy changes that would reduce budget deficits, lawmakers and the public may weigh several factors. The types of changes that people will be willing to accept will depend in part on their view of the proper size of the federal government and the best allocation of its resources. People may also want to consider the distributional implications of proposed changes—that is, who would bear the burden of particular cuts in spending or increases in taxes and who would realize any long-term economic benefits.

In addition, some policy changes would have a large and immediate impact on the budget, whereas others would have effects that would grow considerably over time.

A related consideration is how policy changes would influence the pace of economic recovery and longer-term economic performance. Lawmakers face difficult tradeoffs in deciding how quickly to implement policies to reduce budget deficits.

For example, CBO projects that the significant tax increases and spending cuts that are due to occur in January will probably cause the economy to fall back into a recession next year, but they will make the economy stronger later in the decade and beyond. In contrast, continuing current policies would lead to faster economic growth in the near term but a weaker economy in later years.

Potential policy changes would have different effects on federal borrowing, people's incentives to work and save, and government investment, all of which would affect the nation's output and income during the next few years and over the longer term.

In sum, a wide gap exists between the future cost of the services that the public has become accustomed to receiving from the federal government—especially in the form of benefits for older people—and the tax revenues that the public has been sending to the government to pay for those services.

Because the federal budget is on an unsustainable path under current policies, those policies will need to be changed in significant ways. It is possible to keep tax revenues at their historical average percentage of GDP—but only by making substantial cuts, relative to current policies, in the large benefit programs that aid a broad group of people at some point in their lives. Alternatively, it is possible to keep the policies for those large benefit programs unchanged—but only by raising taxes substantially, relative to current policies, for a broad segment of the population.

Changes in other federal programs can affect the size of the changes needed in taxes or large benefit programs, but they cannot eliminate the basic trade-off between those two parts of the budget.

Chapter 2 – The federal government is confronting significant and fundamental budgetary challenges. If current policies are continued in coming years, the aging of the population and the rising cost of health care will boost federal spending, as a share of the economy, well above the amount of revenues that the federal government has collected in the past. As a result, putting the federal budget on a sustainable path will require significant changes in spending policies, tax policies, or both. The task of addressing those formidable challenges is complicated by the weakness of the economy and the large numbers of unemployed workers, empty houses, and underused factories and offices. Changes that might be made to federal spending or tax policies could have a substantial impact on the pace of economic recovery during the next few years as well as on the nation's output and people's income over the longer term.

Chapter 3 – In 2009, the federal budget deficit (the difference between outlays and revenues) exceeded $1 trillion for the first time, and it has remained above $1 trillion since. Those years also marked the largest the deficit has been as a share of gross domestic product (GDP) in the period since World War II. The budget is not projected to be on a sustainable path under current policy, in the sense that it leads the publicly held debt to continuously grow more quickly than GDP. The timing of deficit reduction remains a difficult issue because of continued weakness in the economy.

If deficits are reduced too quickly, the economy might tip back into recession. If unsustainable deficits persist for too long in the economic recovery, it could crowd out private investment and, in the worst case scenario, investors could refuse to continue to finance deficits that they believed were unsustainable.

As one example of the policy changes that would return the budget to a sustainable path, the Congressional Research Service (CRS) estimates that stabilizing debt as a share of GDP at its 2011 level would require budget deficits averaging 2.8% of GDP over the next 10 years. In dollar terms, the deficit could equal $200 billion in 2013, rising to more than $600 billion from 2015 on.

Under the Congressional Budget Office's (CBO's) current law baseline, the deficit is already on a sustainable path. Under CBO's Alternative Fiscal Scenario, which modifies the current law baseline by assuming that expiring tax provisions and the "doc fix" to Medicare are extended and that the future automatic spending cuts under the Budget Control Act (BCA) do not come into effect, the deficit would decline from more than 9% of GDP in 2011 to 5% of GDP in 2015, then rise to 6% of GDP by 2022. To reduce the deficit to sustainable levels under this scenario would require some combination of spending cuts and tax increases equivalent to roughly $800 billion in 2013, falling to $275 billion in 2015, then rising to $900 billion by 2022.

The recent growth in deficits is the result of spending reaching its highest level as a share of GDP since 1945 and revenues reaching their lowest level as a share of GDP since 1950. Revenues were low because of the recession and because of the temporary extension of expiring tax provisions, such as the "alternative minimum tax (AMT) patch" and "Bush tax cuts."

If these tax cuts are extended again, revenues are estimated to be reduced by about 2.5% of GDP from 2014 on and will remain around their historical average from 2015 on.

Thus far, policy changes to reduce the deficit have targeted mainly discretionary spending. The BCA would reduce discretionary spending by $1.5 trillion and mandatory spending by less than $0.2 trillion over 10 years if automatic cuts are allowed to begin in 2013. Including interest savings, the BCA would reduce the deficit by about 1% of GDP from 2014 on.

Even if these cuts proceed as scheduled, overall spending is projected to rise and remain above its historical average over the next 10 years because of the growth in mandatory spending. Defense, Social Security, and Medicare account for more than half of total spending. Outside of those three programs and net interest, all other spending is about three-quarters the size of the budget deficit in 2012.

Growth in entitlement spending on the elderly drives long-term projections of large budget deficits—by mid-century, outlays on Social Security and health programs would exceed total revenues. Most proposals to reform entitlement programs for the elderly would generate significant budgetary savings in the long run, but little budgetary savings in the short run, partly because most proposals exempt current retirees from reform and partly because the savings from these changes would compound over time.

The US fiscal outlook is not a purely long-term issue, however—deficits are already at unsustainably high levels today.

Chapter 4 - Substantial changes to tax and spending policies are scheduled to take effect in January 2013, significantly reducing the federal budget deficit. According to the Congressional Budget Office's (CBO's) projections, if all of that fiscal tightening occurs, real (inflation-adjusted) gross domestic product (GDP) will drop by 0.5 percent in 2013 (as measured by the change from the fourth quarter of 2012 to the fourth quarter of 2013)—reflecting a decline in the first half of the year and renewed growth at a modest pace later in the year. That contraction of the economy will cause employment to decline and the unemployment rate to rise to 9.1 percent in the fourth quarter of 2013. After next year, by the agency's estimates, economic growth will pick up, and the labor market will strengthen, returning output to its potential level (reflecting a high rate of use of labor and capital) and shrinking the unemployment rate to 5.5 percent by 2018.

Output would be greater and unemployment lower in the next few years if some or all of the fiscal tightening scheduled under current law—sometimes called the fiscal cliff—was removed. However, CBO expects that even if all of the fiscal tightening was eliminated, the economy would remain below its potential and the unemployment rate would remain higher than usual for some time. Moreover, if the fiscal tightening was removed and the policies that are currently in effect were kept in place indefinitely, a continued surge in federal debt during the rest of this decade and beyond would raise the risk of a fiscal crisis (in which the government would lose the ability to borrow money at affordable interest rates) and would eventually reduce the nation's output and income below what would occur if the fiscal tightening was allowed to take place as currently set by law.

In August, CBO presented estimates of the budgetary and economic outcomes that would occur under current law and under an "alternative fiscal scenario" that represents a continuation of many long-standing policies and thus a significant reduction in the amount of fiscal tightening next year. To provide additional information about the sources of that tightening and its effects, this report presents estimates of the budgetary and economic impact of the main changes to current law that would occur under that alternative scenario, as well as estimates of the impact of eliminating various other components of fiscal tightening scheduled for 2013.

In order to focus on the short-term impact of policy decisions, the analysis in this report is based on the assumption that the fiscal tightening would be removed and current policies maintained for two years and that the tightening provided by current law would occur thereafter. (In contrast, CBO's August analysis of the alternative fiscal scenario was based on the assumption that those current policies would be maintained indefinitely.)

In: Federal Deficit Reduction ISBN: 978-1-62417-779-8
Editors: Carl Frankel and Dan Iglehart

Chapter 1

CHOICES FOR DEFICIT REDUCTION[*]

Leigh Angres, Christi Hawley Anthony, Barry Blom and Janet Holtzblatt

SUMMARY

The United States is facing fundamental budgetary challenges. Federal debt held by the public exceeds 70 percent of the nation's annual output (gross domestic product, or GDP)—a percentage not seen since 1950— and a continuation of current policies would boost the debt further. Although debt would decline to 58 percent of GDP in 2022 under the current-law assumptions that underlie the Congressional Budget Office's (CBO's) baseline projections, those projections depend heavily on significant increases in taxes and decreases in spending that are scheduled to take effect at the beginning of January. If, instead, lawmakers maintained current policies by preventing most of those changes from occurring—what CBO refers to as the alternative fiscal scenario—debt held by the public would increase to 90 percent of GDP 10 years from now and continue to rise rapidly thereafter.

Federal debt cannot grow faster than the nation's output indefinitely, and prolonged increases in debt relative to GDP can cause significant long-term damage to both the government's finances and the broader economy. Higher debt leads to larger federal interest payments; making those payments would eventually require some combination of lower

[*] This is an edited, reformatted and augmented version of Congress of the United States, Congressional Budget Office, Publication No. 4569, dated November 2012.

government spending and higher taxes. In addition, increases in debt tend to reduce national saving, leading to more borrowing from abroad and less domestic investment, which in turn reduces the growth of income. Moreover, when debt rises, lawmakers are less able to use tax and spending policies to respond to unexpected challenges, such as economic downturns, natural disasters, or financial crises. Rising debt could itself precipitate a fiscal crisis by undermining investors' confidence in the government's ability to manage the budget, thus making it harder for the government to borrow money at affordable interest rates.

With the population aging and health care costs per person likely to keep growing faster than the economy, the United States cannot sustain the federal spending programs that are now in place with the federal taxes (as a share of GDP) that it has been accustomed to paying. To put the budget on a path that is more likely to be sustainable than if current policies were continued, lawmakers will need to adopt a combination of policies that require people to pay more for their government, accept less in government benefits and services, or both. However, making policy changes that are large enough to shrink the debt relative to the size of the economy—or even to keep the debt from growing—will be a formidable task.

This report reviews the scale and sources of the federal government's budgetary imbalance, various options for bringing spending and taxes into closer alignment, and criteria that lawmakers and the public might use to evaluate different approaches to deficit reduction. The report focuses on CBO's alternative fiscal scenario, rather than on the current-law baseline, to show the size of the policy changes—relative to policies now in place—that would be necessary to put the budget on a more sustainable path.

The discussion builds on estimates that CBO has published previously and, for simplicity, focuses on potential deficit reduction in one year: 2020. Lawmakers could set various deficit reduction goals for that year, such as the following:

- Bringing the federal budget into balance by 2020, which would require policy changes that would reduce the deficit in that year by about $1 trillion relative to the effects of the current policies embodied in CBO's alternative fiscal scenario;
- Keeping debt held by the public the same size relative to GDP at the end of 2020 that it will be early in 2013—roughly 75 percent—which would require deficit reduction of about $500 billion in 2020 compared with the alternative fiscal scenario; or
- Reducing the deficit in 2020 by $750 billion relative to the alternative fiscal scenario, which is roughly the difference between the deficits (excluding interest costs) projected for 2020 in that scenario and in the current-law baseline.

Very few policy changes, taken individually, can shrink the deficit enough to achieve any of those objectives. Ultimately, significant deficit reduction is likely to require a combination of policies, many of which may stand in stark contrast to policies now in place. This report briefly reviews some potential policy changes that lawmakers might consider, showing how far those changes would go toward reducing the deficit in 2020.

The policy options come from CBO's March 2011 report *Reducing the Deficit: Spending and Revenue Options* and from other CBO analyses. They are meant to be illustrative only; many other possible policy changes could be considered.

In evaluating policy changes that would reduce budget deficits, lawmakers and the public may weigh several factors. The types of changes that people will be willing to accept will depend in part on their view of the proper size of the federal government and the best allocation of its resources. People may also want to consider the distributional implications of proposed changes—that is, who would bear the burden of particular cuts in spending or increases in taxes and who would realize any long-term economic benefits.

In addition, some policy changes would have a large and immediate impact on the budget, whereas others would have effects that would grow considerably over time.

A related consideration is how policy changes would influence the pace of economic recovery and longer-term economic performance. Lawmakers face difficult tradeoffs in deciding how quickly to implement policies to reduce budget deficits.

For example, CBO projects that the significant tax increases and spending cuts that are due to occur in January will probably cause the economy to fall back into a recession next year, but they will make the economy stronger later in the decade and beyond. In contrast, continuing current policies would lead to faster economic growth in the near term but a weaker economy in later years.

Potential policy changes would have different effects on federal borrowing, people's incentives to work and save, and government investment, all of which would affect the nation's output and income during the next few years and over the longer term.

In sum, a wide gap exists between the future cost of the services that the public has become accustomed to receiving from the federal government—especially in the form of benefits for older people—and the tax revenues that the public has been sending to the government to pay for those services.

Because the federal budget is on an unsustainable path under current policies, those policies will need to be changed in significant ways. It is possible to keep tax revenues at their historical average percentage of GDP—but only by making substantial cuts, relative to current policies, in the large benefit programs that aid a broad group of people at some point in their lives. Alternatively, it is possible to keep the policies for those large benefit programs unchanged—but only by raising taxes substantially, relative to current policies, for a broad segment of the population.

Changes in other federal programs can affect the size of the changes needed in taxes or large benefit programs, but they cannot eliminate the basic trade-off between those two parts of the budget.

INTRODUCTION

With the federal budget deficit surpassing $1 trillion for the fourth year in a row and federal debt climbing rapidly, the need is growing to address the government's budgetary situation. Major changes to current tax or spending policies will be necessary to put the budget on a more sustainable path, but such changes will require significant trade-offs between deficit reduction and other policy goals.

This report highlights the scale of the nation's budgetary challenges, shows how far some illustrative policy changes that the Congressional Budget Office (CBO) has analyzed in past reports would go toward meeting those challenges, and discusses important factors that policymakers and the public might consider when evaluating budget plans.

HOW BIG ARE PROJECTED U.S. DEFICITS AND DEBT?

To provide a benchmark against which potential changes in law can be measured, CBO constructs so-called baseline projections of what federal revenues and spending will be in the future if current laws generally remain unchanged.

On that basis, the budget deficit is projected to shrink markedly in coming years: from 7.0 percent of gross domestic product ($1.1 trillion) in fiscal year 2012 to 2.4 percent of GDP ($387 billion) in 2014. Between 2015 and 2022, deficits fluctuate in a narrow range, from 0.4 percent to 1.2 percent of GDP, in CBO's baseline projections. With those deficits, debt held by the public is projected to rise from 73 percent of GDP at the end of 2012 to 77 percent in 2014 but then decline relative to the size of the economy, to 58 percent of

GDP in 2022— still higher than the roughly 20 percent to 50 percent range seen between 1957 and 2008.

Those baseline projections, however, are heavily influenced by policy changes that are scheduled to occur under current law—changes that in many cases represent a significant departure from recent policies. To illustrate the budgetary consequences of maintaining the tax and spending policies that have been in effect recently, CBO has also produced budget projections under an alternative fiscal scenario.[1]

That scenario incorporates the following assumptions:

- That all expiring tax provisions (other than the recent reduction in the payroll tax for Social Security), including tax provisions that expired at the end of December 2011, are extended;
- That the parameters of the alternative minimum tax (AMT) are indexed to increase with inflation after 2011 (starting from the 2011 exemption amount);
- That Medicare's payment rates for physicians' services are held constant at their current level; and
- That provisions of the Budget Control Act of 2011 that established automatic enforcement procedures designed to reduce discretionary and mandatory spending beginning in January 2013 do not go into effect, although the law's original caps on discretionary appropriations remain in place.[2]

Under that alternative fiscal scenario, deficits would be much larger during the 2013–2022 period than in CBO's baseline, averaging 4.9 percent of GDP rather than 1.1 percent (see Table 1). With deficits totaling nearly $10 trillion during that decade, debt held by the public would climb to 90 percent of GDP in 2022, the highest percentage since just after World War II. Thus, under that scenario, the United States would quickly head into fiscal territory unfamiliar to it and most other developed nations. Moreover, federal debt would continue to grow over the longer term, more than doubling relative to GDP between 2022 and 2037 (see Figure 1).[3]

This report focuses on the alternative fiscal scenario, rather than on CBO's current-law baseline, to illuminate more clearly the consequences of continuing tax and spending policies that the nation has become accustomed to. Focusing on the alternative scenario also demonstrates the size of the policy changes—relative to policies currently in place—that would be necessary to put the budget on a more sustainable path.

Table 1. Deficits Projected in CBO's Baseline and Under the Alternative Fiscal Scenario

											Total	
	Actual, 2012a	**2013**	**2014**	**2015**	**2016**	**2017**	**2018**	**2019**	**2020**	**2021**	**2022**	**2013-2017**	**2013-2022**
	In Billions of Dollars												
	CBO's August 2012 Baseline												
Revenues	2,449	2,913	3,208	3,541	3,817	4,083	4,328	4,551	4,790	5,039	5,295	17,562	41,565
Outlays	3,538	3,554	3,595	3,754	4,003	4,206	4,407	4,681	4,932	5,183	5,509	19,111	43,823
Deficit	-1,089	-641	-387	-213	-186	-123	-79	-130	-142	-144	-213	-1,549	-2,258
Debt Held by the Public at the End of the Year	11,280	12,064	12,545	12,861	13,144	13,371	13,536	13,746	13,964	14,181	14,464	n.a.	n.a
	Alternative Fiscal Scenario												
Revenues	2,449	2,583	2,825	3,111	3,361	3,596	3,808	3,996	4,196	4,399	4,608	15,476	36,483
Outlays	3,538	3,621	3,748	3,921	4,193	4,430	4,678	4,999	5,298	5,599	5,970	19,913	46,457
Deficit	**-1,089**	**-1,037**	**-924**	**-810**	**-832**	**-833**	**-870**	**-1,003**	**-1,102**	**-1,200**	**-1,362**	**-4,437**	**-9,975**
Debt Held by the Public at the End of the Year	11,280	12,460	13,478	14,391	15,321	16,258	17,215	18,298	19,477	20,749	22,181	n.a.	n.a.
	As a Percentage of Gross Domestic Product												
	CBO's August 2012 Baseline												
Revenues	15.8	18.4	19.6	20.3	20.6	20.7	20.8	20.9	21.1	21.2	21.4	20.0	20.6
Outlays	22.8	22.4	21.9	21.5	21.6	21.4	21.2	21.5	21.7	21.8	22.3	21.7	21.7
Deficit	-7.0	-4.0	-2.4	-1.2	-1.0	-0.6	-0.4	-0.6	-0.6	-0.6	-0.9	-1.8	-1.1
Debt Held by the Public at the End of the Year	72.6	76.1	76.6	73.8	70.8	67.9	65.2	63.2	61.4	59.8	58.5	n.a.	n.a.
	Alternative Fiscal Scenario												
Revenues	15.8	16.3	17.2	17.8	18.1	18.3	18.3	18.4	18.5	18.5	18.6	17.6	18.1
Outlays	22.8	22.8	22.9	22.5	22.6	22.5	22.5	23.0	23.3	23.6	24.1	22.6	23.0

											Total	
	Actual, 2012a	**2013**	**2014**	**2015**	**2016**	**2017**	**2018**	**2019**	**2020**	**2021**	**2022**	**2013-2017**	**2013-2022**
	In Billions of Dollars												
Deficit	-7.0	-6.5	-5.6	-4.6	-4.5	-4.2	-4.2	-4.6	-4.8	-5.1	-5.5	-5.0	-4.9
Debt Held by the Public at the End of the Year	72.6	78.6	82.3	82.5	82.5	82.5	82.9	84.1	85.7	87.5	89.7	n.a.	n.a.
Memorandum: Deficit: Alternative Fiscal Scenario Minus CBO's August 2012 Baseline													
In billions of dollars	n.a.	-396	-537	-597	-647	-711	-791	-873	-960	-1,056	-1,149	-2,888	-7,717
As a percentage of GDP	n.a.	-2.5	-3.3	-3.4	-3.5	-3.6	-3.8	-4.0	-4.2	-4.5	-4.6	-3.3	-3.8

Sources: Congressional Budget Office; Department of the Treasury.

Notes: The alternative fiscal scenario incorporates the assumptions that all expiring tax provisions (other than the payroll tax reduction), including those that expired at the end of December 2011, are instead extended; that the alternative minimum tax is indexed for inflation after 2011 (starting at the 2011 exemption amount); that Medicare's payment rates for physicians' services are held constant at their current level; and that the automatic enforcement procedures specified by the Budget Control Act of 2011 do not take effect. Outlays under that scenario also include the incremental interest costs associated with projected additional borrowing.
n.a. = not applicable.

a. Numbers for 2012 were derived from information reported in Department of the Treasury, *Final Monthly Treasury Statement of Receipts and Outlays of the United States Government for Fiscal Year 2012 Through September 30, 2012, and Other Periods* (September 2012), www.fms.treas.gov/mts/index.html.

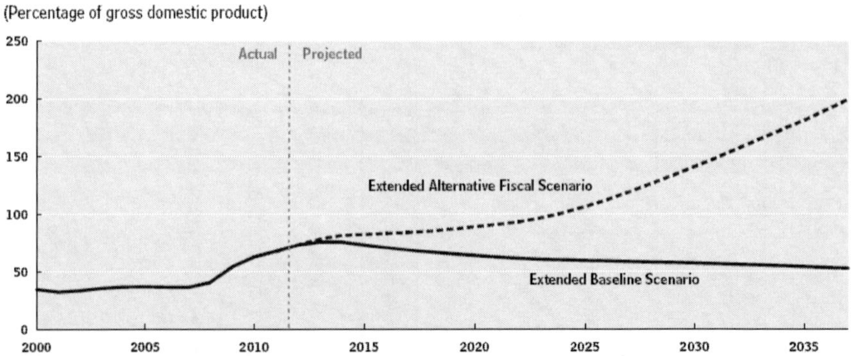

Source: Congressional Budget Office, *The 2012 Long-Term Budget Outlook* (June 2012).

Note: The extended baseline scenario generally adheres closely to current law, following CBO's 10-year baseline budget projections through 2022 and then extending the baseline concept for the rest of the long-term projection period. The extended alternative fiscal scenario incorporates the assumptions that all expiring tax provisions (other than the payroll tax reduction), including those that expired at the end of December 2011, are instead extended; that the alternative minimum tax is indexed for inflation after 2011 (starting at the 2011 exemption amount); that Medicare's payment rates for physicians' services are held constant at their current level; and that the automatic enforcement procedures specified by the Budget Control Act of 2011 do not take effect. Outlays under that scenario also include the incremental interest costs associated with projected additional borrowing.

Figure 1. Federal Debt Held by the Public Under CBO's Long-Term Budget Scenarios.

WHAT FACTORS ARE PUTTING INCREASING PRESSURE ON THE BUDGET?

The aging of the baby-boom generation portends a significant and sustained increase in coming years in the share of the population that will receive benefits from Social Security and Medicare and long-term care services financed through Medicaid. Moreover, per capita spending on health care is likely to continue to grow faster than per capita spending on other goods and services for many years. (The size of the future gap between those growth rates is uncertain and will undoubtedly vary from year to year. On average, over the past 25 years, health care costs per person have grown about 11/2 percentage points faster per year than potential GDP per person.)[4]

Without significant changes in the laws governing Social Security, Medicare, and Medicaid, those factors will boost federal outlays as a percentage of GDP well above the average of the past several decades—a conclusion that applies under any plausible assumptions about future trends in demographics, economic conditions, and health care costs. Unless the laws governing those programs are changed—or the increased spending is accompanied by sufficiently lower spending on other programs, sufficiently higher revenues, or a combination of the two— deficits will be much larger in the future than they have tended to be in the past.

For example, under the alternative fiscal scenario, which generally reflects a continuation of recent policies, federal spending would average 23 percent of GDP over the coming decade and equal 24 percent of GDP by 2022, CBO projects, compared with an average of 21 percent over the past 40 years (1972 to 2011). Revenues would remain close to 18 percent of GDP, about their average over the past four decades. As a result, the deficit under the alternative fiscal scenario would equal about 5 percent of GDP in 2020 and larger percentages thereafter— significantly greater than the 3 percent average seen in recent decades. (By comparison, in CBO's current-law baseline, federal spending is projected to average 22 percent of GDP over the next 10 years and revenues nearly 21 percent of GDP, both above their 40-year averages. Projected deficits in the baseline average about 1 percent of GDP over that period.)

To illustrate the sources of the large deficit increases under the alternative fiscal scenario, it is useful to compare the experience of the past few decades with CBO's projections for several broad categories of the budget: spending for Social Security, Medicare, and other major health care programs; all other spending (except interest on federal debt); net interest outlays; and revenues (see Figure 2).

Spending for Social Security and Major Health Care Programs

With the oldest baby boomers now at retirement age, the number of people age 65 or older is projected to increase by about one-third in the next 10 years. In addition, health care costs per person are projected to continue rising, and the Affordable Care Act (ACA) will substantially increase the number of people who receive federal assistance in obtaining health care.[5] As a result, outlays for Social Security and the federal government's major health care programs (Medicare, Medicaid, the Children's Health Insurance Program, and subsidies offered through new health insurance exchanges and related spending) are projected to total 11.5 percent of GDP in 2020 under the alternative fiscal scenario, up from 9.6 percent in 2012 and an average of 7.1 percent over the past 40 years.[6]

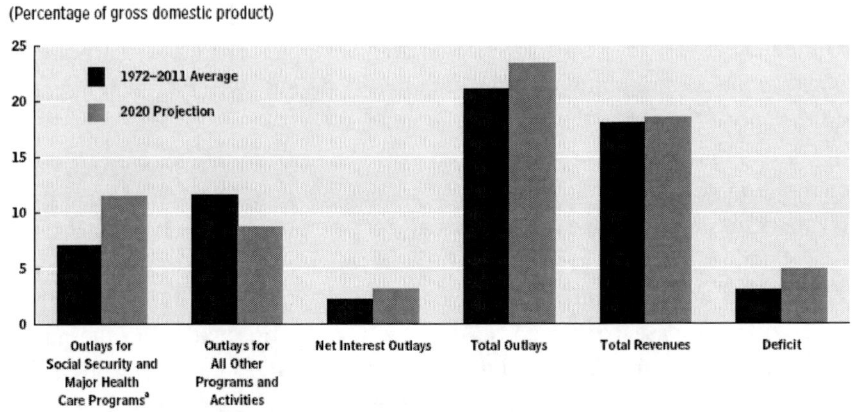

Source: Congressional Budget Office.

Note: The alternative fiscal scenario incorporates the assumptions that all expiring tax provisions (other than the payroll tax reduction), including those that expired at the end of December 2011, are instead extended; that the alternative minimum tax is indexed for inflation after 2011 (starting at the 2011 exemption amount); that Medicare's payment rates for physicians' services are held constant at their current level; and that the automatic enforcement procedures specified by the Budget Control Act of 2011 do not take effect. Outlays under that scenario also include the incremental interest costs associated with projected additional borrowing.

a. The federal government's major health care programs consist of Medicare, Medicaid, the Children's Health Insurance Program, and subsidies offered through new health insurance exchanges and related spending.

Figure 2. Components of the Federal Budget in 2020 Under the Alternative Fiscal Scenario, Compared with Their Averages Since 1972.

Spending for Social Security alone will total 5.3 percent of GDP in 2020, CBO projects (see Table 2 on page 8), up from 4.9 percent in 2012 and an average of 4.3 percent over the past four decades. Net outlays for major health care programs are projected to equal 6.3 percent of GDP in 2020 under the alternative fiscal scenario, compared with 4.7 percent in 2012.[7] Federal outlays for such health care programs averaged 2.7 percent during the past 40 years. The increase in spending for health care programs is much greater than the increase for Social Security because the health care programs are affected by rising costs per beneficiary and legislated expansions in benefits, as well as by the aging of the population.

Most of the outlays for Social Security and major health care programs are spent on benefits for people over age 65, with smaller shares for blind and disabled people and for nonelderly able-bodied people. Specifically, CBO estimates that more than four-fifths of Social Security spending in 2020 will go toward benefits for retired workers and their dependents and survivors; the remainder will go toward benefits for disabled workers and their spouses and children. In addition, despite the significant expansion of federal support for health care for lower-income people enacted in the ACA, about half of spending for major health care programs in 2020 will finance care for people over age 65, CBO projects. Another quarter will finance health care for blind and disabled people, and the remaining quarter will finance care for able-bodied nonelderly people.

Other Noninterest Spending

Besides Social Security and major health care programs, the federal government spends money on a wide variety of programs and services—including national defense, income security programs, retirement benefits for federal civilian employees and military personnel, transportation, health research, education, law enforcement, agriculture, and many other activities. Unlike spending for Social Security and major health care programs, spending on all of those activities would decline considerably relative to the size of the economy over the next 10 years under both the alternative fiscal scenario and CBO's baseline. Taken together, outlays for that broad collection of other programs and activities would equal 8.7 percent of GDP in 2020 under the alternative fiscal scenario, compared with an average of 11.6 percent over the past 40 years.[8]

Thus, the United States is already on track to significantly shrink the federal resources dedicated to activities other than Social Security and major health care programs to a much smaller share of the economy than they have represented for the past several decades. Such reductions may prove unpopular once they take effect or, in the case of discretionary programs, once policymakers determine the size of the cuts to specific benefits and services. As a result, those reductions may be difficult to carry out and maintain.

Table 2. Budget Projections for 2020 in CBO's Baseline and Under the Alternative Fiscal Scenario

	CBO's August 2012 Baseline		Alternative Fiscal Scenario	
	Billions of Dollars	Percentage of GDP	Billions of Dollars	Percentage of GDP
Revenues				
Individual income taxes	2,542	11.2	2,055	9.0
Social insurance taxes	1,412	6.2	1,412	6.2
Corporate income taxes	473	2.1	424	1.9
Other	363	1.6	305	1.3
Total Revenues	4,790	21.1	4,196	18.5
Outlays				
Mandatory spending				
Social Security	1,202	5.3	1,202	5.3
Medicare[a]	750	3.3	793	3.5
Medicaid	514	2.3	514	2.3
Other major health care programs[b]	117	0.5	117	0.5
Other mandatory spending	523	2.3	566	2.5
Subtotal	3,104	13.7	3,190	14.0
Discretionary spending Defense	696	3.1	750	3.3
Nondefense	620	2.7	653	2.9
Subtotal	1,316	5.8	1,403	6.2
Net interest	512	2.3	704	3.1
Total Outlays	4,932	21.7	5,298	23.3
Deficit	-142	-0.6	-1,102	-4.8
Debt Held by the Public at the				
End of the Year	13,964	61.4	19,477	85.7

Source: Congressional Budget Office.

Notes: The alternative fiscal scenario incorporates the assumptions that all expiring tax provisions (other than the payroll tax reduction), including those that expired at the end of December 2011, are instead extended; that the alternative minimum tax is indexed for inflation after 2011 (starting at the 2011 exemption amount); that Medicare's payment rates for physicians' services are held constant at their current level; and that the automatic enforcement procedures specified by the Budget Control Act of 2011 do not take effect. Outlays under that scenario include the incremental interest costs associated with projected additional borrowing.

GDP = gross domestic product.

a Outlays for Medicare include offsetting receipts from premium payments and from payments by states from savings on Medicaid prescription drug costs.

b Other major health care programs consist of the Children's Health Insurance Program and subsidies offered through new health insurance exchanges and related spending.

Net Interest and Total Spending

Net interest payments by the federal government would equal 3.1 percent of GDP in 2020 under the alternative fiscal scenario, compared with an average of 2.2 percent during the past 40 years. Interest payments would be greater as a share of GDP because the government's indebtedness would be larger relative to the size of the economy.

The substantial decline in other federal spending relative to GDP would not be enough to offset the increased burden on the budget from rising outlays for Social Security, major health care programs, and interest payments. Putting those pieces together, CBO projects that total outlays under the alternative fiscal scenario would equal 23.3 percent of GDP in 2020, compared with an average of 21.0 percent since 1972.[9]

Revenues

Under the alternative fiscal scenario, the increase in spending as a share of GDP (relative to the historical average) would not be matched by a corresponding increase in revenues. Federal revenues would amount to 18.5 percent of GDP in 2020, CBO estimates, slightly above the 17.9 percent average recorded over the past 40 years.[10] The alternative scenario incorporates the continuation of certain tax policies that have been in place for a number of years—specifically, the extension of all expiring tax provisions (other than the payroll tax cut) and the indexing of the AMT for inflation after 2011. If those policies are not continued, and instead the changes scheduled to occur under current law take place, revenues will rise to 21.1 percent of GDP in 2020, by CBO's estimate.

One way to understand the size of the gap between revenues and outlays under the alternative fiscal scenario is to compare revenues with spending for a few key programs. CBO projects that, in total, spending for Social Security, Medicare, other major health care programs, defense, and interest payments under that scenario would nearly equal all of the government's revenues in 2020 and would exceed them from 2022 onward—leaving no revenues to cover any other federal activities, such as income security programs, retirement benefits for federal civilian and military employees, transportation, research, education, law enforcement, and many other programs (see Figure 3).

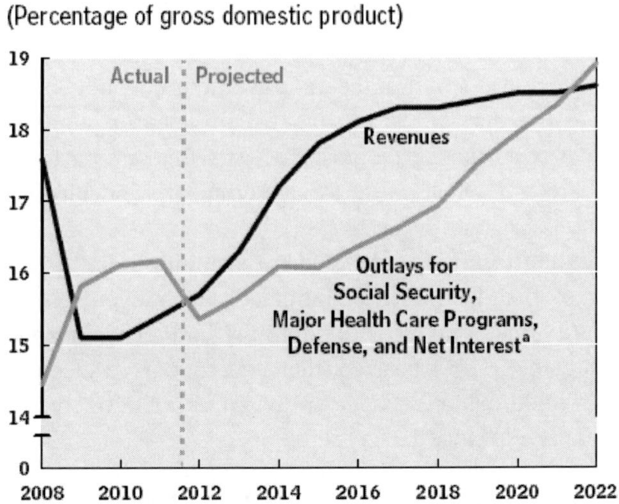

Note: The alternative fiscal scenario incorporates the assumptions that all expiring tax provisions (other than the payroll tax reduction), including those that expired at the end of December 2011, are instead extended; that the alternative minimum tax is indexed for inflation after 2011 (starting at the 2011 exemption amount); that Medicare's payment rates for physicians' services are held constant at their current level; and that the automatic enforcement procedures specified by the Budget Control Act of 2011 do not take effect. Outlays under that scenario also include the incremental interest costs associated with projected additional borrowing.

a. The federal government's major health care programs consist of Medicare, Medicaid, the Children's Health Insurance Program, and subsidies offered through new health insurance exchanges and related spending.

Figure 3. Outlays for Major Programs Compared with Total Revenues Under the Alternative Fiscal Scenario.

WHAT ARE THE CONSEQUENCES OF RISING FEDERAL DEBT?

If annual budget deficits were large enough to keep federal debt increasing relative to GDP for the next decade and beyond, that growing debt would have significant harmful effects on the budget and the economy—which in turn would cause debt to grow even faster. In particular, rising debt would have the following consequences:

- *Higher federal spending on interest payments.* For example, about half of the projected increase in net interest outlays between 2012 and 2020 under the alternative fiscal scenario is attributable to the greater debt that would result from the policies in that scenario. Such an increase in interest costs would eventually require higher taxes, a decrease in government benefits and services, or some combination of the two.
- *A reduction in national saving.* That reduction would lead to more borrowing from abroad and less domestic investment, which in turn would decrease income in the United States relative to what it would be otherwise.
- *Limits on policymakers' ability to use tax and spending policies to respond to unexpected challenges, such as economic downturns, natural disasters, or financial crises.* With policymakers' options limited, unexpected events could have worse effects on the economy and people's well-being than they would otherwise.
- *An increase in the likelihood of a fiscal crisis.* During such a crisis, investors would lose confidence in the government's ability to manage its budget, and the government would thereby lose the ability to borrow funds at affordable interest rates.

Under the alternative fiscal scenario, those negative consequences would worsen during the coming decade as debt grew faster than GDP. Because debt would rise indefinitely as a percentage of GDP and never stabilize, the alternative scenario is ultimately unsustainable.

Other trajectories for federal debt are possible—for example, stabilizing the debt relative to the size of the economy at the level projected for early 2013. Such an outcome would result in lower interest payments and higher national income than under the alternative fiscal scenario. However, a stable but high level of debt would still leave the country with less ability to respond to unexpected developments and at greater risk of a fiscal crisis than if the debt was stabilized at a lower level. It is impossible to predict with any confidence whether or when a fiscal crisis might occur in the United States; in particular, there is no identifiable level of debt relative to GDP that indicates that a crisis is likely or imminent. At any given time, the risk of such a crisis depends not only on the debt levels and economic conditions in the United States and other countries at the time but also on expectations about budgetary and economic developments in the future. All else being equal, however, the greater the amount of federal debt, the greater the risk of a fiscal crisis.[11]

WHAT KINDS OF POLICY CHANGES COULD LEAD TO A MORE SUSTAINABLE BUDGETARY PATH?

If lawmakers want to put the federal budget on a path that is more likely to be sustainable than the one that would occur under current policies, they will have to change those policies in at least one of the following ways:

- Make major reductions in the benefits that people receive when they get older, relative to the benefits envisioned in current policies;
- Substantially decrease the other activities of the federal government, relative to the size of the economy, beyond the reductions that are already projected to occur; or
- Raise revenues significantly above their historical average as a percentage of GDP.

Under the alternative fiscal scenario, the deficit would total $1.1 trillion (4.8 percent of GDP) in 2020, CBO projects, and federal debt would be on an upward trajectory as a percentage of GDP.[12] Such continually rising debt would eventually prove untenable. In the rest of this report, CBO examines policy changes that could produce a fiscal path that is more likely to be sustainable than the alternative fiscal scenario.

Possible Targets for Deficit Reduction

Although the nation cannot sustain continuous growth in debt as a percentage of GDP indefinitely, people may differ about what is a sustainable path. Thus, the precise amount of deficit reduction required to put the budget on such a path is not clear, and various objectives are possible:

- One potential goal would be to balance the federal budget by 2020, which would require policy changes that would save roughly $1 trillion in that year relative to the alternative fiscal scenario (with interest savings contributing the remaining deficit reduction). Maintaining a balanced budget in the years after 2020 would put federal debt on a steadily declining path relative to GDP.
- Another possible goal would be to have debt held by the public equal the same percentage of GDP at the end of 2020 that it will early in

2013: roughly 75 percent. Achieving that goal would require deficit reduction (excluding interest savings) of about $500 billion in 2020.

- An objective midway between those two goals would be to reduce the deficit projected for 2020 by $750 billion relative to the alternative fiscal scenario—roughly the difference between the deficits projected for 2020 in that scenario and in CBO's current-law baseline (excluding the difference in interest costs). Reductions of that magnitude would keep future deficits stable at a relatively small percentage of GDP and thus would put debt on a slightly downward-sloping trajectory relative to GDP, as would occur under the baseline.

Many other budgetary goals are also possible. For the potential objectives listed above, depending on the path chosen to meet the goal, total noninterest deficit reduction over the 10-year period from 2013 to 2022 would range between $3 trillion and $8 trillion relative to the alternative fiscal scenario.

Overview of Options to Reduce the Deficit

To provide some perspective about the scope and scale of policy changes that would be necessary to put the budget on a more sustainable path, this section presents various options for reducing mandatory or discretionary spending or increasing revenues. Many of the policy changes come from a collection of budget options that CBO

publishes periodically to help inform lawmakers about possible fiscal choices. (The most recent volume, published in March 2011, included more than 100 options for cutting federal spending or raising revenues.)[13] Other policy options discussed here come from other recent CBO analyses.

The rough estimates of the options' effect on the deficit in 2020 are based on hypothetical proposals and are presented for illustrative purposes only. In most cases, CBO has not updated its estimates of the options to reflect its current baseline budget projections. Estimates of legislative proposals related to these options might differ from the estimates shown here because of specific details that might be incorporated into proposed legislation, or because of revised baseline projections, or for other reasons. Moreover, some of the options interact in ways that would cause their total effect to differ from the sum of the individual effects described here.

The options discussed in this report are intended to reflect a range of possibilities rather than a ranking of priorities or a comprehensive list. Many of the policy changes could be implemented in ways that would achieve more or less budgetary savings than are reported here. Moreover, numerous other policies that would decrease spending or increase revenues to a greater or lesser extent could be considered as lawmakers work to reduce the deficit. For example, various proposals for future budgetary savings have included establishing a premium support system in Medicare, which would involve setting a fixed federal contribution toward the cost of premiums, with beneficiaries bearing any difference between that amount and actual premiums. That policy change is not included here because CBO did not publish an estimate for such an option in its March 2011 volume and does not currently have an estimate for such a proposal.

The timing for implementing policy changes would affect the total amount of deficit reduction in any given year. The more the deficit was reduced in earlier years, the greater the impact that reduction would have in lowering the government's future interest costs. The more that changes were delayed until later, the larger those changes would ultimately have to be to achieve similar deficit reduction.

For simplicity, this analysis focuses on a single year, 2020, but the policy changes would have varying budgetary effects over time. For instance, options that were phased in by applying only to people below a specific age would tend to have effects that continued to grow over time, compared with options that were fully implemented right away. In addition, options that changed the annual growth rate of benefits would tend to have effects that grew more quickly over time (as the differences in growth rates compounded) than would options that changed the level of benefits. Similarly, options that changed the way tax brackets are indexed for inflation would have effects that continued to increase over time, compared with options that immediately changed tax rates.

The options presented in this report illustrate how challenging it would be to shrink the deficit by as much as $500 billion, $750 billion, or $1 trillion in 2020. Very few policy changes that CBO has examined in the past are large enough, by themselves, to accomplish a sizable portion of that deficit reduction. Moreover, many of the options that would have a substantial budgetary impact would require large numbers of people to pay more in taxes or receive less in government benefits or services; others would shift significant costs to state governments, leaving them to decide whether to increase the taxes they collect or to cut the benefits or services they provide.

CBO's March 2011 volume of budget options summarizes some advantages and disadvantages of each of the options. This report does not repeat those points, but a later section discusses broad criteria that policymakers and the public might use in making choices about deficit reduction.

Another approach to deficit reduction, which could be combined with choosing specific policy changes, would be to adopt "fiscal rules"—specific numerical targets for spending, revenues, deficits, or debt in future years—and to create procedures that would take effect if those targets were not met. However, experience in the United States suggests that fiscal rules are not a substitute for making difficult budgetary choices and that if consensus about budgetary goals erodes, fiscal rules will not necessarily prevent lawmakers from spending more or taxing less than the rules allow. Rather, fiscal rules are most useful in formalizing goals and enforcing budgetary choices to which policymakers have already agreed and generally remain committed. (For more about fiscal rules and their application, see the appendix.)

Options That Would Reduce Mandatory Spending

Outlays for programs that are not funded through the annual appropriation process make up roughly 60 percent of the federal government's noninterest spending. Under both current law and the alternative fiscal scenario, mandatory outlays are projected to grow more rapidly near the end of the 2013–2022 period, largely because of the aging of the population and rising spending for health care. That rapid growth will occur even though mandatory spending for activities other than Social Security and major health care programs is projected to decline as a percentage of GDP. By 2020, mandatory outlays are projected to total $3.2 trillion, or 14.0 percent of GDP, under the alternative fiscal scenario.

CBO has previously analyzed a number of options to decrease mandatory spending (see Table 3 on page 14). Those options can be grouped in three categories:

- *Health care programs.* Of the health-related proposals for which CBO has published an estimate, the one with the largest savings would repeal provisions of the Affordable Care Act that expand health insurance coverage (while leaving other provisions of that law unchanged). That option would decrease spending for major health care programs by nearly 15 percent in 2020 and would reduce the deficit by roughly $150 billion in that year, according to estimates by CBO and the staff of the Joint Committee on Taxation (JCT).[14] The option would also increase the number of people without health insurance coverage by an estimated 29 million in 2020. Various other changes to health care programs for which CBO has published estimates would save between $5 billion and $50 billion each in 2020 (not counting interactions with other potential policy changes).

- *Social Security.* Of the proposals involving Social Security for which CBO has published estimates, the three with the largest savings would raise the ages at which people qualify for benefits or reduce the size of their initial benefit. Any of those changes would decrease outlays by about $30 billion in 2020.
- *Other mandatory programs.* Of the proposals in this category for which CBO has published an estimate, the one with the largest savings involves allowing the automatic enforcement procedures in the Budget Control Act to take effect. Doing so would reduce outlays for a large number of mandatory programs, including some health-related programs, by a total of $15 billion in 2020. A second proposal in this category involves changing the rate structure for student loans, which would reduce mandatory outlays by $10 billion in 2020.

The options listed in Table 3 would generally decrease the amount paid to beneficiaries of various programs or reduce payments to state governments or health care providers. Some of the options would also encourage changes in the systems for financing or providing health care, create incentives for people to work longer or save more before they retire, or have various other economic and social consequences.

If policymakers wanted to reduce the deficit by $750 billion in 2020, the savings from enacting all of the options shown in Table 3 would achieve about 80 percent of that goal and would result mainly from changes to major health care programs and Social Security.[15] (If interactions among the various policies were taken into account, the total savings would be smaller.) Some of those options would save significantly more in later years as the affected population increased and health care costs continued to rise. Also, many of the policy changes could be implemented in ways that would produce greater budgetary savings, although such alternatives would generally impose larger burdens on program beneficiaries, state governments, or health care providers than the versions shown here.

Mandatory programs other than Social Security, Medicare, and Medicaid are a good deal smaller than those three programs, so the options for changing them that CBO has analyzed in the past would generally produce smaller savings. Specifically, CBO projects that spending on other mandatory programs will total about $700 billion in 2020.[16] Thus, generating hundreds of billions of dollars in savings from those programs would require very large percentage cuts in spending.

Among options discussed in recent CBO publications, altering the interest rate structure for student loans and reducing income-eligibility limits and maximum benefits for the Supplemental Nutrition Assistance Program (formerly known as Food Stamps) would together save about $15 billion in 2020. CBO has also analyzed a number of changes to smaller mandatory programs, such as those involving agriculture: prohibiting new enrollment in the Department of Agriculture's Conservation Stewardship Program, limiting enrollment in the Conservation Reserve Program, reducing the premium subsidy in the crop insurance program, and reducing the share of a farmer's base acreage eligible for direct payments from the department. Each of those options would result in savings smaller than those shown in Table 3; together, they would save less than $15 billion in 2020. For the most part, the individual options presented in Table 3 would involve spending cuts of less than 10 percent for specific programs in 2020. Larger reductions in particular programs are possible. For example, converting the Supplemental Nutrition Assistance Program to a block grant to states that would grow more slowly than the spending projected under current law could result in greater savings. However, CBO has not recently estimated the budgetary impact of specific large changes of that sort.

Options That Would Reduce Discretionary Spending

Nearly 40 percent of federal noninterest outlays stem from budget authority provided in annual appropriation acts. Those discretionary outlays pay for a wide variety of federal activities, including most programs related to national defense, transportation, elementary and secondary education, veterans' health care, international affairs, and law enforcement. Before the enactment of the Budget Control Act of 2011, CBO's baseline projections for discretionary spending reflected the assumption that the most recent year's budget authority would be provided in each future year, with adjustments for projected inflation. The Budget Control Act established caps on discretionary funding that are set to constrain such spending significantly. The automatic enforcement procedures contained in that law, which are scheduled to take effect in January, are set to reduce discretionary funding even further.[17]

Table 3. Approximate Potential Savings in 2020 from Selected Options to Reduce Mandatory Spending

Other Mandatory Programs	**Approximate Potential Deficit Reduction in 2020 (Billions of dollars)**
Allow the automatic enforcement procedures in the Budget Control Act to take effecth	15
Change the interest rate structure for student loans	10
Reduce income eligibility limits and maximum benefits for the Supplemental Nutrition Assistance Programi	5

Source: Congressional Budget Office.

Note: The options shown here are the same as those included in Congressional Budget Office, *Reducing the Deficit: Spending and Revenue Options* (March 2011), unless otherwise noted below. Options with savings of at least $20 billion in 2020 are rounded to the nearest $10 billion; options with savings below that amount are rounded to the nearest $5 billion. Updated estimates of any of the options could result in more or less savings in 2020 than shown here. In addition, some of the options interact with one another, meaning that the sum of the estimates shown in the table would not equal the savings if all of the options were enacted at the same time.

a This option would affect revenues as well as outlays; the total effect on the deficit is shown here.

b See Congressional Budget Office, letter to the Honorable John Boehner providing an estimate for H.R. 6079, the Repeal of Obamacare Act (July 24, 2012).

c This estimate does not incorporate the effect of the Supreme Court's decision in *National Federation of Independent Business v. Sebelius,* which established that the expansion of Medicaid in the Affordable Care Act is optional for states.

d See Congressional Budget Office, *Raising the Ages of Eligibility for Medicare and Social Security* (January 2012).

e This option would also affect discretionary spending.

f In this option, cost-of-living adjustments for inflation would be made using the chained consumer price index for all urban consumers (chained CPI-U) instead of the consumer price index for urban wage earners and clerical workers (CPI-W). CBO estimates that over the next decade, the chained CPI-U is likely to grow at an average annual rate that is 0.25 percentage points less than the growth rate of the CPI-W. If this option was applied to other federal benefit programs, it would reduce the deficit by an additional $10 billion in 2020.

g See Congressional Budget Office, *Policy Options for the Social Security Disability Insurance Program* (July 2012).

h This estimate, which includes the option's effects on health care programs but excludes its effects on discretionary spending, comes from CBO's August 2012 baseline projections. See Congressional Budget Office, *An Update to the Budget and Economic Outlook: Fiscal Years 2012 to 2022* (August 2012).

i See Congressional Budget Office, *The Supplemental Nutrition Assistance Program* (April 2012).

Under the alternative fiscal scenario—which includes the original spending caps in the Budget Control Act but not the reductions stemming from the automatic enforcement procedures—discretionary outlays would total $1.4 trillion in 2020. That amount would equal 6.2 percent of GDP, down from an estimated 8.3 percent in 2012 and well below the average (8.7 percent of GDP) seen over the past 40 years. Indeed, under that alternative scenario, the government's discretionary spending would represent a smaller share of the economy by 2020 than it has for nearly all of the past 40 years. (Discretionary spending would be even lower if funding for the war in Afghanistan and similar activities diminished; both CBO's baseline and the alternative fiscal scenario incorporate the assumption that such spending will continue at the amount appropriated for 2012, with increases for inflation.) Thus, significant reductions in discretionary outlays as a share of GDP are already embodied in the alternative fiscal scenario. One broad policy change that would generate a large amount of additional deficit reduction relative to the alternative fiscal scenario involves maintaining appropriations at the amounts designated for 2013 (as originally provided for in the Budget Control Act). If appropriations covered by the discretionary spending caps were maintained at their 2013 amounts rather than increasing modestly each year, total discretionary outlays in 2020 would be about $145 billion lower than under the alternative fiscal scenario: $75 billion lower for defense programs and $70 billion lower for nondefense programs (see Table 4). Maintaining appropriations at their 2013 level would represent a cut of 12 percent relative to the amount of funding that would result if those appropriations grew at the projected rate of inflation. Another broad option would be to allow the automatic enforcement procedures of the Budget Control Act to take effect in January (which is not assumed in the alternative fiscal scenario). Those automatic procedures would reduce defense and nondefense discretionary spending in 2020 by a total of $88 billion relative to the amounts projected in the alternative fiscal scenario.[18] Although the savings from such broad options can be estimated in the aggregate, lawmakers would ultimately have to make detailed program-by-program decisions about how to apportion such reductions. Specific options for cutting discretionary spending that CBO has examined recently would produce much smaller budgetary savings than would those broad options—or most of the options for changing mandatory spending or revenues discussed elsewhere in this report— because the amounts of funding provided for most individual discretionary programs are relatively small. Estimates for most of those specific options were based on appropriations provided for 2011, but they can be used to approximate savings relative to more recent appropriations.

Table 4. Approximate Potential Savings in 2020 from Selected Options to Reduce Discretionary Spending

	Approximate Potential Deficit Reduction in 2020 (Billions of dollars)
Defense Discretionary Programs	
Keep appropriations at the level originally set by the Budget Control Act for 2013[a]	75
Allow the automatic enforcement procedures in the Budget Control Act to take effect[a,b]	54
Limit the TRICARE benefit for military retirees and their dependentsc	14
Reduce the across-the-board adjustment for federal civilian employees' pay Increase cost sharing for pharmaceuticals under TRICAREb	4 2
Cap increases in military basic pay	2
Nondefense Discretionary Programs	
Keep appropriations at the level originally set by the Budget Control Act for 2013[a]	70
Allow the automatic enforcement procedures in the Budget Control Act to take effect[a,b]	34
Limit highway funding to expected highway revenues	11
Reduce the across-the-board adjustment for federal civilian employees' pay	6
Eliminate federal grants for wastewater and drinking water infrastructure	4
Reduce funding for the National Institutes of Health	4
Increase payments by tenants in federally assisted housing	4
Increase fees for aviation security	2
Eliminate the transit Starts programs	2
Reduce Department of Energy funding for energy technology development	2
Eliminate certain grant programs for elementary and secondary education	2
Eliminate grants to large and medium-sized hub airports Restrict Pell grants to needier studentsb	1 1
Eliminate funding for national community service programs Finance the Food Safety and Inspection Service through feesd	1 1

Source: Congressional Budget Office.

Note: The options shown here are the same as those included in Congressional Budget Office, *Reducing the Deficit: Spending and Revenue Options* (March 2011), unless otherwise noted below. Estimates are rounded to the nearest $1 billion. Updated estimates of any of these options could result in more or less savings in 2020 than shown here.

a This estimate is calculated from CBO's August 2012 baseline projections. For more details about those projections, see Congressional Budget Office, *An Update to the Budget and Economic Outlook: Fiscal Years 2012 to 2022* (August 2012).

b This option would also affect mandatory spending.

c This option would also affect mandatory spending and revenues.

d The fees collected under this option could be recorded in the budget as offsetting collections (discretionary), offsetting receipts (usually mandatory), or revenues, depending on the specific language used to establish the fees.

The specific options that would produce the largest savings in discretionary spending in 2020—$10 billion to $14 billion (see Table 4)—are the following:

- Limiting the health care benefits provided to military retirees and their dependents through the Department of Defense's TRICARE program (which combines access to military hospitals and clinics with coverage for services received from civilian health care providers),
- Limiting the amount of highway funding to match the highway revenues expected to be collected at current tax rates,[19] and
- Reducing annual across-the-board salary adjustments for both defense and nondefense civilian employees.

Enacting all of the specific changes shown in Table 4 would reduce discretionary spending by a total of about $60 billion (or 4 percent) in 2020, compared with amounts of funding that would rise with inflation. That total would not be enough to keep discretionary budget authority in line with the caps originally set in the Budget Control Act; greater reductions would be required just to comply with those caps, and even larger cuts would be necessary to comply with the automatic enforcement procedures that are scheduled to take effect in January.

Because of the caps on budget authority established by that law (even without the automatic reductions set to occur in January), discretionary outlays would be $86 billion lower in 2020 than they would be if the funding provided for 2012 was continued in later years with increases for inflation; that difference would mean a 6 percent decrease in the real (inflation-adjusted) resources available for a large collection of government programs and activities. However, even if 2012 funding levels continued, with adjustments for inflation, the resources available for some programs could be insufficient to continue current policies. For example, if current enrollment rules stay the same, the cost of veterans' health care will rise more rapidly than inflation, CBO projects.[20] Similarly, keeping award amounts for Pell grants at their current levels will require greater funding than the 2012 appropriation increased for inflation. Maintaining such programs in their present form without increasing deficits would require even larger cuts to other discretionary programs.

In 2012, just over half of discretionary outlays went to defense programs—mainly for operations and maintenance, military personnel, and procurement. Cuts in defense spending could be targeted toward personnel levels, pay rates, and benefits; training and supplies; day-to-day operating and administrative costs; procurement, operation, and maintenance of existing weapon systems; or research and development aimed at producing more advanced weapon systems.[21] However, large and sustained reductions in funding in those areas could have substantial effects on military capabilities and thus could require changes in broad strategic objectives, with significant implications for national security.[22]

Similarly, large cuts in nondefense discretionary spending could affect a broad range of activities—covering such areas as education, transportation, housing subsidies, health-related research, and public health. Decisions about specific programs would have effects beyond their impact on the federal budget. For example, many federal programs provide funds to state and local governments. Reducing federal support for such programs would force other levels of government to make decisions about decreasing the scope of the programs, increasing their own funding, or some combination of the two.

Options That Would Increase Revenues

Lawmakers could raise revenues by modifying existing taxes—either by increasing tax rates or by expanding tax bases (the measures, such as personal or corporate income, on which taxes are assessed). For example, various tax bases could be expanded by eliminating or curtailing tax expenditures (the many exclusions, deductions, exemptions, credits, and other features of the tax system that resemble government spending programs by providing assistance to specific activities, entities, or groups of people).[23] Alternatively, lawmakers could impose new taxes on income, consumption, or particular activities. All of those approaches would have effects not only on the amount of revenues collected but also on economic activity, the distribution of the tax burden among households, and the complexity of the tax system.

CBO's March 2011 volume of budget options and more recent publications contain a variety of alternatives for raising revenues. Those options, which were analyzed by JCT and CBO, include changes to income tax rates and the income tax bases for individuals and corporations, expansions of the Social Security tax base, increases in excise taxes, and several new taxes (see Table 5).[24] Many of the revenue options would make broad enough changes to the tax code to have larger effects on the deficit than many of the changes to individual spending programs discussed above.

Table 5. Approximate Potential Savings in 2020 from Selected Options to Increase Revenues

	Approximate Potent Deficit Reduction in 2020 (Billions of dollars)
Reverse Changes in Law Assumed in the Alternative Fiscal Scenario[a]	
Let tax cuts originally enacted in 2001, 2003, and 2009 expire as scheduled; let estate and gift tax provisions enacted in 2010 expire as scheduled; and do not index the AMT for inflation	550
Extend certain tax cuts originally enacted in 2001, 2003, and 2009 for taxpayers below a specific income threshold; extend estate and gift tax provisions enacted in 2010; and index the AMT for inflation[b]	110
Modify Existing Taxes[c]	
Limit the tax benefit of itemized deductions to 15 percent	150
Eliminate the deduction for state and local taxes	110
Increase the payroll tax rate for Medicare Hospital Insurance by 1 percentage point	80
Increase the maximum taxable earnings for the Social Security payroll taxd	60
Gradually eliminate the mortgage interest deduction	50
Tax Social Security and Railroad Retirement benefits in the same way as distributions from defined-benefit pensions	50
Accelerate and modify the excise tax on high-cost health care coverage	40
Include employer-paid premiums for income replacement insurance in employees' taxable incomed	40
Extend the period for depreciating the cost of certain investments	30
Increase excise taxes on motor fuels by 25 cents per gallon	30
Include investment income from life insurance and annuities in taxable income	30
Curtail the deduction for charitable contributions	30
Replace the tax exclusion for interest income on state and local bonds with a direct subsidy for the issuer	30
Repeal the deduction for domestic production activities	20
Expand Social Security coverage to include newly hired state and local government employees	20
Use an alternative measure of inflation to index some parameters of the tax codee	10
Establish New Taxes[c]	
Impose a 5 percent value-added tax on a broad base	320
Impose a price on emissions of greenhouse gases	140

Sources: Congressional Budget Office; Joint Committee on Taxation.

Table 5. (Continued)

Notes: The options shown here are the same as those included in Congressional Budget Office, *Reducing the Deficit: Spending and Revenue Options* (March 2011), unless otherwise noted below. Estimates are rounded to the nearest $10 billion. Many of the options interact with one another (for example, limiting the tax benefit of itemized deductions would reduce the savings from eliminating specific deductions). In addition, the estimates for the first two options are based on more recent economic and technical assumptions than the estimates for the other options and reflect savings relative to the alternative fiscal scenario rather than changes from current law (as is the case for the other options). As a result, the sum of the estimates shown in the table would not equal the savings if all of the options were enacted at the same time.

AMT = alternative minimum tax.

[a] The estimates in this section are of savings relative to the alternative fiscal scenario, which incorporates the assumption that legislative action extends title I of the Tax Relief, Unemployment Insurance Reauthorization, and Job Creation Act of 2010 (which extended for 2011 and 2012 income tax provisions enacted in 2001, 2003, and 2009) and title III of that act (which modified estate and gift taxation for 2010 through 2012). The alternative fiscal scenario also incorporates the assumption that the exemption amount for the AMT (which was increased through the end of 2011) is extended at its higher amount and, together with the AMT's tax brackets, is indexed for inflation after 2011. In addition, the treatment of nonrefundable personal credits (which was also continued through the end of 2011) is assumed to be extended. These estimates are based on CBO's August 2012 economic and technical assumptions. See Congressional Budget Office, *An Update to the Budget and Economic Outlook: Fiscal Years 2012 to 2022* (August 2012), Table 1-5.

[b] Under this option, the tax cuts would expire as scheduled only for couples filing joint tax returns with income over $250,000 per year and for single taxpayers with income over $200,000. The option also includes the assumptions that the AMT would be indexed for inflation and that the estate and gift tax provisions enacted in 2010 would be extended. See Congressional Budget Office, *An Update to the Budget and Economic Outlook: Fiscal Years 2012 to 2022* (August 2012), Table 1-5.

[c] The estimates in this section are of savings relative to CBO's current-law baseline and do not incorporate the assumptions of the alternative fiscal scenario. The estimates are based on CBO's January 2011 economic and technical assumptions. See Congressional Budget Office, *Reducing the Deficit: Spending and Revenue Options* (March 2011).

[d] This option would affect mandatory spending as well as revenues; the total effect on the deficit is shown here.

[e] In this option, the federal government would use the chained consumer price index for all urban consumers (chained CPI-U) to adjust various parameters of the tax code for inflation instead of using the traditional CPI-U. CBO estimates that over the next decade, the chained CPI-U is likely to grow at an average annual rate that is 0.25 percentage points less than the growth rate of the traditional CPI-U.

Among the options to alter existing taxes, the ones that would have the greatest impact on revenues—an additional $110 billion to $550 billion in 2020—are the following:

- Letting various tax cuts expire as scheduled and not indexing the alternative minimum tax for inflation,
- Limiting the extent to which taxes can be reduced through itemized deductions to 15 percent of the deductions' value, and
- Eliminating the income tax deduction for payments of state and local taxes.

The option with the largest revenue impact—allowing the tax cuts originally enacted in 2001, 2003, and 2009 to expire as scheduled; allowing estate and gift tax provisions enacted in 2010 to expire as scheduled; and not indexing the AMT for inflation after 2011—would reduce the deficit in 2020 by about $550 billion relative to the alternative fiscal scenario. That option would thus provide about three-quarters of the deficit reduction needed to cut the deficit by $750 billion in 2020 relative to the alternative fiscal scenario, for example. (Those policies are already embodied in CBO's current-law baseline projections.) If those tax cuts expired as scheduled only for high-income taxpayers but were extended for everyone else, the estate and gift tax provisions were extended, and the AMT was indexed for inflation, the amount of deficit reduction in 2020 would be much smaller: about $110 billion. Many other changes to tax policies are possible, some of which would yield even more revenues and some a good deal less. In many cases, choices about tax policies involve significant trade-offs between deficit reduction and other policy goals, such as providing incentives for economic growth or distributing the tax burden fairly among households. For example, raising tax rates would reduce the deficit but also lessen people's incentives to work and save. Alternatively, expanding tax bases would reduce the deficit and generally have a smaller negative effect, or even a positive effect, on how efficiently the economy operates.

WHAT CRITERIA MIGHT BE USED TO EVALUATE POLICY CHANGES?

Reducing the deficit by $500 billion, $750 billion, or $1 trillion in 2020 relative to the alternative fiscal scenario would be a formidable task.

As lawmakers consider changes in budget policies, many factors may play a role in their decisions. The size and composition of the changes they choose to make to federal spending and revenues will affect the total amount and types of output produced and consumed in the United States, the distribution of that output among different segments of society, and people's well-being.

The rest of this report discusses several factors that policymakers and the public might consider in evaluating budget plans:

- How big would the government be?
- How would the government's resources be allocated among various priorities?
- How much would deficits be reduced in the next 10 years and beyond?
- What would the economic impact be in the short term as well as in the medium and long term?
- Who would bear the burden of proposed changes in tax and spending policies?

The way that people think about those criteria, and the relative importance they attach to such considerations, will vary according to their individual preferences.

How Big Would the Government Be?

The approach that lawmakers choose to take toward deficit reduction will be determined partly by their view of the proper size and scope of the federal government.

One approach, for example, would be to provide government services and benefits so that total spending remained at about 23 percent of GDP (the percentage estimated for 2012 and the average during the coming decade under the alternative fiscal scenario). With spending at that level, reducing the deficit would require significantly higher taxes than the nation has been accustomed to paying. A starkly different approach would be to keep revenues at roughly 18 percent of GDP (the average percentage over the past 40 years and the average during the coming decade under the alternative fiscal scenario).

With revenues at that level, significant spending cuts would be required to shrink the deficit. Many other objectives—either within the range defined by those two approaches or outside that range—are also possible. Moreover, the size and scope of the government depend not just on the magnitude of total spending and revenues relative to GDP but also on the nature of spending programs and the tax code, the government's regulatory activities, and other factors.

How Would the Government's Resources Be Allocated?

Fiscal policies are judged not only by their effects on the sustainability of the federal budget but also by the extent to which they accomplish other national goals.

Under current law, the United States is on track to have a federal budget that will look very different from budgets of the past: As the population ages, a much larger share of federal spending will go toward benefits for older people and a much smaller share will go toward other types of benefits and services. If federal spending for purposes other than Social Security, health care, and net interest declined sharply relative to the size of the economy over the next decade—as it would under either CBO's current-law baseline or the alternative fiscal scenario (see Figure 4)— the services that the government provides in the areas of national defense, income security, education, and transportation would probably be cut substantially compared with other goods and services in the economy.

Conversely, if significant reductions were made to spending for Social Security or major health care programs, the average benefits received by older people would probably be much smaller than they would be under current policies.

Changes to the tax code can also affect the way in which federal resources are allocated to achieve various social goals. For example, if revenues were increased by curtailing the number or size of deductions or credits in the tax system, the support that the government provides for various private activities could be cut substantially.

Thus, in considering policies aimed at reducing deficits, policy-makers and the public will need to make judgments about what types of programs and activities are appropriate for the government to carry out or subsidize and about what priorities they attach to various types of spending and to various benefits conveyed through the tax system.

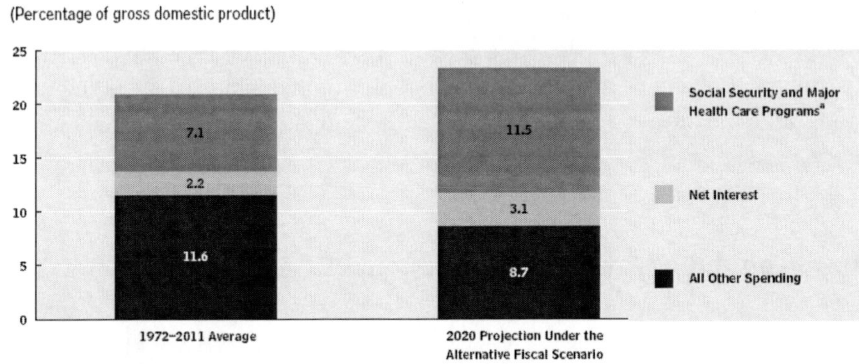

Source: Congressional Budget Office.

Note: The alternative fiscal scenario incorporates the assumptions that all expiring tax provisions (other than the payroll tax reduction), including those that expired at the end of December 2011, are instead extended; that the alternative minimum tax is indexed for inflation after 2011 (starting at the 2011 exemption amount); that Medicare's payment rates for physicians' services are held constant at their current level; and that the automatic enforcement procedures specified by the Budget Control Act of 2011 do not take effect. Outlays under that scenario also include the incremental interest costs associated with projected additional borrowing.

a. The federal government's major health care programs consist of Medicare, Medicaid, the Children's Health Insurance Program, and subsidies offered through new health insurance exchanges and related spending.

Figure 4. Components of Federal Spending in 2020 Under the Alternative Fiscal Scenario, Compared with Their Averages Since 1972.

How Much Would Deficits Be Reduced in the Next 10 Years?

Policymakers will also need to make judgments about how much deficit reduction should be accomplished within the next 1, 5, or 10 years. For any given amount of deficit reduction, looking at different slices of the budget—such as spending for Social Security and major health care programs, other noninterest spending, and revenues—illustrates how large policy changes would need to be to bring about that reduction. For instance, cutting the deficit by $750 billion in 2020 relative to the alternative fiscal scenario could require changes of the following sizes:

- If the deficit reduction came entirely from Social Security and major health care programs, that reduction would need to total about 30 percent of the nearly $2.6 trillion projected to be spent on those programs under the alternative fiscal scenario in 2020.

- If the deficit reduction came entirely from other noninterest spending (including national defense), it would have to total nearly 40 percent of the estimated $2.0 trillion in such spending projected for 2020 under the alternative fiscal scenario.
- If the deficit reduction came entirely from taxes, revenues would need to rise by almost 20 percent from the $4.2 trillion estimated to be collected in 2020 under the alternative fiscal scenario.

If the policy changes involved two of those three categories rather than just one, they would still need to be large. For example, if half of the $750 billion in deficit reduction came from Social Security and major health care programs and half came from revenues, that combination would require a cut of 14 percent in spending for those programs and an increase of 9 percent in tax collections. The changes would be one-third smaller or larger if the deficit reduction target for 2020 was $500 billion or $1 trillion.

How much the deficit is cut in the next few years will have a number of consequences. The longer that significant deficit reduction is deferred, the larger the government's accumulated debt will be (with its associated costs and risks), and the greater the policy changes will need to be when deficit reduction begins. Conversely, the sooner that the deficit is cut, the less time that households, businesses, and state and local governments will have to plan and adjust their behavior. In addition, the timing of the steps taken to put fiscal policy on a sustainable course will affect different generations differently and will have a substantial impact on the economy (as discussed below).

How Much Would Deficits Be Reduced in the Long Term?

Because the aging of the population and the continuing growth of health care costs have consequences well beyond the next 10 years, the fiscal challenges facing the nation are long term in nature. CBO projects that under the alternative fiscal scenario, spending on major federal health care programs alone would grow from roughly 5 percent of GDP today to more than 10 percent in 25 years (see Figure 5) and would continue to increase thereafter. Spending on Social Security is projected to rise much less sharply, from about 5 percent of GDP today to more than 6 percent in 2037 and subsequent decades.[25] Unless those programs are changed, or the increased spending is accompanied by some combination of sufficiently lower spending on other programs and sufficiently higher revenues, deficits will be much larger in the future than they have tended to be in the past.

Thus, putting the nation on a sustainable fiscal path requires steps that will reduce or constrain deficits over the long term. Some policy options would have much greater budgetary effects after the next 10 years than they would during the next decade. For example, if changes in the full retirement age for Social Security or in the eligibility age for Medicare were phased in gradually or did not apply to people currently age 55 or older, they would have much larger effects in future decades than in the next several years.[26] Similarly, if the growth rate of Medicare spending per beneficiary was effectively restrained through some policy change, the budgetary effects would compound over time, and the long-term savings would be much larger than the short-term savings. As another example, reducing initial Social Security Disability Insurance benefits by 15 percent (as shown in Table 3 on page 14) would cut spending by about 10 percent relative to the total benefits that would be paid under current law in 2020 but by about 15 percent relative to current-law benefits in 2035. Changes that reduced benefits in that way would have larger effects not only on future budget deficits but also on the future income of affected individuals.

What Would the Economic Impact Be in the Short Term?

Under current law, the deficit is set to shrink by about $450 billion (or 3.0 percent of GDP) between fiscal years 2012 and 2013, CBO estimates, mostly because of scheduled increases in taxes and, to a lesser extent, scheduled reductions in spending. In CBO's view, that fiscal tightening will cause real GDP to decrease slightly in calendar year 2013—the result of a contraction in the first half of the year and a modest expansion in the second half.[27] Given the pattern of past recessions (as identified by the National Bureau of Economic Research), such an economic contraction in the first half of 2013 would probably be judged a recession. That projected effect of sharp deficit reduction on short-term economic growth under current law is one illustration of the difficult tradeoffs that lawmakers face in deciding how quickly to implement policies to reduce the deficit.

Lawmakers might address the short-term economic challenge by eliminating or reducing the fiscal tightening that is scheduled to occur next year without tackling the fiscal challenges that remain in the future. That approach would not be sustainable indefinitely, however, and it would have substantial economic costs over the longer term. Alternatively, policymakers could move rapidly to address the longer-term budgetary problem by allowing the full measure of fiscal tightening now embodied in current law to take effect next year, although that course would have substantial economic costs during the year.

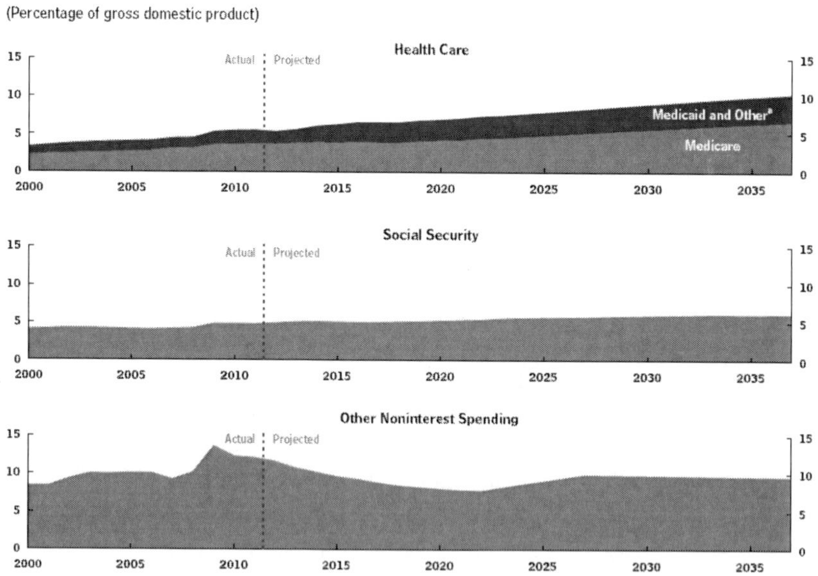

Source: Congressional Budget Office, *The 2012 Long-Term Budget Outlook* (June 2012).

Note: The extended alternative fiscal scenario incorporates the assumptions that all expiring tax provisions (other than the payroll tax reduction), including those that expired at the end of December 2011, are instead extended; that the alternative minimum tax is indexed for inflation after 2011 (starting at the 2011 exemption amount); that Medicare's payment rates for physicians' services are held constant at their current level; and that the automatic enforcement procedures specified by the Budget Control Act of 2011 do not take effect. Outlays under that scenario also include the incremental interest costs associated with projected additional borrowing.

a. Other major health care programs consist of the Children's Health Insurance Program and subsidies offered through new health insurance exchanges and related spending.

Figure 5. Components of Noninterest Spending Under the Extended Alternative Fiscal Scenario.

Intermediate possibilities would be to extend some, but not all, current policies indefinitely (perhaps with offsetting changes in other policies); to phase out current policies more gradually; or to extend or enact certain policies for a limited period. In particular, if policymakers wanted to minimize both the short-term economic costs of shrinking the deficit very quickly and the longer-term costs of allowing large deficits to persist, they could enact a combination of changes in tax and spending policies that would increase the deficit in 2013 relative to what it would be under current law but that would reduce deficits later in the decade relative to what would occur if current policies were extended. That approach, however, would allow a greater amount of federal debt to accumulate and might raise doubts about whether longer-term deficit reduction would actually take place. Households, businesses, state and local governments, and participants in the financial markets would be more likely to believe that the future deficit reduction would truly take effect if the future policy changes were specific and widely supported.[28]

What Would the Economic Impact Be in the Medium and Long Term?

The effects of deficit reduction on the economy beyond the next few years would depend on the specific policy changes that were made to achieve that reduction. A decrease in federal borrowing would increase the stock of private capital (such as factories, vehicles, and computers) and thereby raise future output and income relative to what they would be otherwise. However, the policy changes used to reduce federal borrowing could have other effects on future output and income as well.

For example, increasing revenues by raising marginal tax rates on labor (the rates that would apply to an additional dollar of a taxpayer's income from work) would reduce people's incentive to work and therefore reduce the amount of labor supplied to the economy, whereas increasing revenues to a similar extent by broadening the tax base would probably have a smaller negative effect, or even a positive effect, on the amount of labor supplied.[29] A reduction in the labor supply, by itself, would decrease output in the medium and long term. Similarly, increasing marginal tax rates on capital would tend to reduce people's incentive to save and thus the amount of private saving, which would also decrease output in the longer term (excluding the effects of less federal borrowing). Alternatively, cutting government benefit payments, such as unemployment insurance or retirement benefits, would probably strengthen people's incentives to work and save, although the impact would depend on the nature of the cuts. Another alternative, reducing federal investment in such things as infrastructure and education, would decrease future output (also excluding the effects of less federal borrowing).

Therefore, to assess the overall economic impact of a deficit reduction plan in the medium and long term, the favorable effects of less federal borrowing must be combined with the effects of the specific changes in taxes and spending.[30] However, even if lawmakers reduced federal budget deficits through policy changes that worsened incentives to work and save and that trimmed federal investment, the net impact on the nation's long-term output and income would probably be positive.

For example, CBO recently compared the economic outcomes that would result from the policies included in the current-law baseline and the alternative fiscal scenario.[31] Relative to the alternative fiscal scenario, adherence to current law would probably increase output and income later in this decade and beyond. The expiration of the tax provisions would raise tax rates on capital income and labor earnings, which would decrease private saving and the supply of labor; those responses, by themselves, would reduce future output. However, the effects of those responses would probably be outweighed by the impact of the substantial decrease in budget deficits, which, by itself, would increase future output by a growing amount over time. Hence, by CBO's estimates, the policy changes scheduled to occur under current law would, on balance, have a positive medium- and long-term effect on the economy. Conversely, if lawmakers decided to maintain current policies and extend the expiring tax provisions, output and income would be lower in the medium and long term than they would be under current law, CBO estimates.[32]

To the extent that deficit reduction led to greater economic output in the medium and long term, the accompanying increases in taxable income would reduce the deficit further by raising revenues. In addition, the decrease in federal borrowing would lower interest rates, which would cut the government's interest payments. Thus, somewhat smaller policy changes would be needed to achieve any particular target for deficit reduction than calculations that exclude such macroeconomic effects would imply. However, the additional deficit reduction that would result from those economic effects would probably be small relative to the underlying impact of the policy changes. Specifically, CBO has estimated that the increase in taxable income and the reduction in interest rates that would result from a gradual decrease in deficits over the coming decade would generate additional deficit reduction in

2020 that would be roughly 10 percent of the size of the deficit reduction in that year resulting directly from policy changes.[33]

Some policymakers have proposed broadly restructuring the individual income tax system, the corporate income tax system, or both as part of an effort to reduce deficits.

If such restructuring strengthened the economy in the medium and long term, it would increase taxable income and thereby reduce deficits. However, the deficit reduction would probably be small relative to the gap between federal spending and revenues in the alternative fiscal scenario.

As an illustration, suppose that tax restructuring lowered the effective marginal tax rate on labor earnings by 5 percentage points (roughly the increase in that rate scheduled to occur between 2011 and 2015). Suppose also that the revenue loss was made up exactly—without incorporating any macroeconomic effects—by expanding the tax base. According to a rough estimate by CBO, the resulting increase in GDP would probably boost tax revenues by less than half a percent of GDP, or less than $100 billion in 2020.[34] Changes to the tax code that reduced effective marginal tax rates to a lesser extent and also had no net impact on deficits in the absence of any macroeconomic effects would generally have smaller effects on GDP and tax revenues. However, the impact of any particular plan for tax restructuring would depend not only on the size of changes in marginal tax rates but also on the distribution of those changes among taxpayers and the impact on the allocation of resources in the economy.

Who Would Bear the Burden of Proposed Changes in Tax and Spending Policies?

Different types of tax increases and spending cuts would affect various groups of people to different extents. Those effects could be direct, such as changes in the amount of taxes that people owe or the amount of benefits or services they receive, or indirect, such as changes that alter the state of the economy. Indirect effects are harder to anticipate because they depend on the behavior of many different participants in the economy.

Most changes in taxes and spending programs would affect how tax burdens and government benefits and services are distributed among people at different income levels. In addition, many such changes would alter the relative tax burdens of, and benefits received by, people who have similar income but who differ in other ways. Policy changes might also influence the distribution of taxes and spending among generations.

Under current law, the federal tax system is progressive, meaning that average tax rates rise with income. In 2009, households in the bottom one-fifth (quintile) of the income distribution—who had an average before-tax income of $23,500, including transfer payments such as Social Security benefits—paid a total of about 1 percent of their income in federal taxes (counting individual income taxes, payroll taxes, corporate income taxes, and excise taxes). Households in the middle quintile, with average before-tax income of $64,300, paid 11 percent; and households in the highest quintile, with average before-tax income of $223,500, paid 23 percent. Within the top quintile, average tax rates were higher for higher-income groups: For instance, households in the top 1 percent of the income distribution had an average tax rate of about 29 percent.[35]

Policy changes that increased revenues would probably affect the distribution of the tax burden, but the effects would depend on the type of tax raised and the nature of the increase. Raising income tax rates for higher-income people would make the tax system more progressive. By contrast, increasing most excise taxes—such as those on tobacco or gasoline—would boost the relative tax burdens of lower-income people, who tend to spend a greater proportion of their income on those items. Alternatively, taxes could be raised in such a way as to maintain the current distribution of the tax burden.

Cuts in spending programs would also affect households differently depending on their income. For example, reducing maximum benefits in the Supplemental Nutrition Assistance Program would increase burdens on the program's beneficiaries, who have low income. As another example, raising the full retirement age for Social Security would reduce people's lifetime benefits and would be particularly burdensome for recipients with low income, who tend to rely heavily on Social Security benefits. Such a policy change could be especially difficult for people who could not adjust their work patterns or qualify for Social Security Disability Insurance benefits in response to the change. Other cuts in government benefits or services could have different effects on people with lower or higher income.

Some policy changes that would reduce deficits would affect people with similar income differently. For instance, reducing or eliminating the child tax credit would lessen the economic well-being of people who have dependent children compared with that of people at similar income levels who do not; and eliminating the deduction for state and local taxes would increase tax payments more for people who live in states with high taxes. As another example, some observers gauge the fairness of highway spending by considering the share of funding that comes from taxes paid by highway users rather than from general taxpayer funds, or the share of funding that comes from people in rural versus urban areas. Policy changes can also be evaluated in terms of how they affect different generations. Deficit reduction policies that took effect now would generally increase burdens on people living today. Depending on the specific policy choices, future generations might also receive fewer government benefits and services or pay higher taxes; in some cases, those effects could be greater than the effects on current generations. However, future generations would also benefit from a larger economy and greater income in the longer term if deficits in the next several years were lower than would otherwise be the case.

APPENDIX: ARE FISCAL RULES A USEFUL TOOL FOR ACHIEVING BUDGETARY GOALS?

One way that some governments attempt to manage their budgets is by setting numerical limits— known as fiscal rules—on budget totals, such as spending, revenues, or deficits. According to the International Monetary Fund (IMF), few countries had fiscal rules until the 1990s, when the accumulation of publicly held debt led more governments to look to such rules to achieve fiscal sustainability.[1] By early 2012, 76 of the IMF's 188 member countries had either national rules, supranational rules, or both. Numerous other countries are actively considering such rules. The U.S. government has implemented fiscal rules and other constraints on budgetary decisions in the past and continues to employ them in the current budget process. Merely adopting a fiscal rule is not likely to improve budgetary outcomes.[2] In particular, experience in the United States and elsewhere suggests that fiscal rules are not a substitute for making difficult choices about the budget. Rather, fiscal rules appear to be useful for enforcing budgetary goals when there is a consensus about those goals and about the policy changes needed to meet them. Rules can make it harder for policymakers to succumb to pressure to stray from agreed-upon policy decisions.[3] But when consensus about budgetary goals erodes, rules will not necessarily stand in the way of policymakers who want to spend more or tax less than the rules allow.

Adopting a fiscal rule requires policymakers to decide about a wide range of possible attributes of the rule.[4] One of the most important of those attributes is transparency—in accounting, forecasting, and institutional arrangements. Misrepresenting the true size and timing of future fiscal obligations can seriously undermine a rule. Hence, the presence of supporting institutions, such as audit institutions and independent fiscal agencies, can enhance the effectiveness of rules. Perhaps equally important is a rule's enforceability. Although the legal status of fiscal rules can vary—some are constitutional, some legislative, and some simply stated agreements—the consequences of noncompliance, in whatever form they may take, should be agreed to in advance.

Types of Fiscal Rules

Fiscal rules can apply to various parts of a budget. *Balance, surplus,* or *deficit rules* operate through numerical limits on the budget's bottom line, specifying that spending should not exceed revenues by a particular amount over a given period. Many countries have tried to use a simple annual balanced budget rule, but such a rule gives governments little flexibility to respond to economic weakness by increasing spending or decreasing taxes.[5]

More complex balanced budget rules aim to provide such flexibility through a cyclically adjusted or structural balance rule, which allows for the full operation of "automatic stabilizers" (the automatic ways in which revenues and outlays respond to developments in the economy), although such rules do not allow for new legislation that provides fiscal stimulus. Other rules require budgetary targets to be met over the course of a business cycle and allow for additional adjustments in response to economic conditions. Simple balanced budget rules also give governments little leeway to respond to other unexpected domestic and international challenges. Therefore, some versions of balanced budget rules allow for exceptions when a large percentage of legislators vote for them.

Expenditure rules usually set limits on either total spending, primary spending (which excludes interest costs), or specific categories of spending. Such limits can apply to the amount of spending—in absolute terms or as a percentage of gross domestic product (GDP)—or to the growth rate of spending. *Revenue rules* generally set ceilings on the amount or growth rate of revenues. They are extremely rare among national governments.

Debt rules set either an explicit limit or a target for publicly held debt, whether as a percentage of GDP or in absolute terms. Like balanced budget rules, debt rules give policymakers little flexibility to respond to economic weakness and other challenges, unless specific provisions are included to provide that flexibility. (In many cases, debt rules can even exacerbate economic weakness.)

Experiences with Fiscal Rules at the Federal Level in the United States

Since the 1980s, the federal budget process in the United States has involved a changing collection of rules focused on deficit control. Those rules have taken the form of deficit targets, spending caps, and pay-as-you-go (PAYGO) procedures, which apply to certain types of legislation and attempt to restrict a net increase in the deficit. (PAYGO procedures usually are not classified as fiscal rules under the traditional definition; in a broader sense, however, PAYGO rules are meant to provide a fiscal constraint and thus are included in this discussion.)

Experience in the United States indicates that such budget procedures are much better at enforcing deficit reduction agreements already in place than at forcing such agreements to be reached. Budget procedures that highlight and penalize deviations from agreements can be helpful, but they work only to the extent that lawmakers choose to enforce them; they have not been effective as a stand-alone substitute for specific policy measures.

The Balanced Budget and Emergency Deficit Control Act of 1985 (popularly known as Gramm-Rudman-Hollings) was enacted with the goal of reducing the deficit to a specified level each year until spending was in balance with revenues. If the law's annual deficit targets were not met, automatic across-the-board spending cuts (known as sequestration) were supposed to take effect. Although deficits shrank somewhat in the late 1980s, they exceeded the statutory targets, in some years by large margins. Nevertheless, no significant sequestration was ever implemented.

Part of the reason for that outcome was that the targets— both those set in 1985 and the revised targets adopted a few years later—were not linked to any agreement on the policy changes needed to meet them. Moreover, the targets did not make allowances for worsening economic conditions or other complicating factors, such as the savings and loan crisis of the late 1980s and early 1990s. Thus, there was a strong incentive to adopt overly optimistic economic assumptions in the calculations used to determine whether the deficit target for the year had been exceeded. For those reasons, actual deficits remained above the targets while the law was in effect.[6]

The Budget Enforcement Act of 1990 (BEA) contained a set of deficit-reducing policy changes that had been agreed to at a 1990 budget summit; it also created new processes to enforce budgetary discipline. The law's procedures did not force further reductions in deficits or require policymakers to adopt new policies to compensate for unrealized expectations about the economy. Instead, the BEA set annual caps on discretionary budget authority and the outlays resulting from that budget authority. It also established a PAYGO procedure requiring that Congressional actions that affected revenues or mandatory spending not add to the deficit. Deficits shrank steadily from 1993 through 1997 and were followed by budget surpluses from 1998 through 2001— in large part because of a surge in tax revenues stemming mainly from robust economic growth as well as from further deficit reduction measures such as those enacted in the Omnibus Budget Reconciliation Act of 1993 and the budget deal of 1997.[7] The amount of federal debt held by the public declined as a percentage of GDP for most of the years that the BEA was in effect. Many observers agree that as long as a consensus remained to rein in budget deficits, the discretionary spending caps and PAYGO requirements in the BEA helped achieve that goal.[8] But when deficits gave way to surpluses, the spending caps were overridden in the appropriation process, and new laws affecting mandatory spending and revenues were enacted with significant costs and no offsetting savings. Lawmakers allowed the BEA to expire in 2002. In the absence of statutory requirements between 2002 and 2009, the House and Senate often adopted rules through budget resolutions and other measures that attempted to enforce PAYGO requirements.

In 2010, the Congress and the President established new statutory PAYGO requirements and directed the Administration to enforce compliance with them through a sequestration mechanism. The following year, lawmakers made another attempt to incorporate a fiscal rule in the budget process by enacting the Budget Control Act of 2011. That law created caps on discretionary budget authority; it also provided for automatic spending cuts if deficit reduction legislation originating from a bipartisan committee of legislators was not enacted by January 15, 2012. The committee was unable to produce a legislative proposal, so the automatic cuts are part of current law and are scheduled to begin in January 2013. Some lawmakers have proposed adjusting or eliminating the reductions, however. Throughout the past few decades, some lawmakers have supported imposing fiscal rules through amendments to the Constitution. The proposed rules have generally involved a balanced budget constraint, sometimes accompanied by a spending limit or revenue limit. The Congress has never approved such an amendment, however.

Experiences with Selected Fiscal Rules in Europe

European nations, and the European Union (EU) as a whole, have also experimented with fiscal rules. In many cases, the rules themselves have been insufficient to achieve the desired budgetary outcomes. Where they have been effective, transparency and enforceability have been key components of their success. To qualify for entry into Europe's Economic and Monetary Union, known as the euro zone, countries were required to meet fiscal targets defined in the Treaty of Maastricht and later enshrined in the Stability and Growth Pact (SGP). Those targets included keeping annual budget deficits at no more than 3 percent of GDP and gross debt at no more than 60 percent of GDP (or approaching the debt target at a satisfactory pace).[9]

Although many countries made an initial push to meet the targets when the euro zone was established in 1999, those efforts were scaled back over time once the euro had been fully introduced and membership in the zone had been granted.[10] Some countries have circumvented the deficit limit with overly optimistic economic forecasts and creative accounting. Such actions have reduced the pressure to make substantial short- and medium-term changes in policies. Using overly optimistic forecasts enabled countries to project favorable budgetary outcomes and then blame poor results on the economy. Some nations have also used accounting measures to exclude certain types of spending—such as government support for public companies—from calculations of budget deficits.[11] In addition, in the wake of the global financial crisis and recession, some countries have found it extremely difficult or impossible to meet the targets specified earlier. (At the same time, the SGP's rules have restricted some governments' ability to respond to those economic problems.) The euro zone's rules have also been plagued by enforcement problems, for several reasons.[12] First, review by the Economic and Financial Affairs Council—a body of national ministers from all member states that has power to issue warnings to members and impose fines as a recourse—has been an ineffective means of oversight. Second, financial penalties for noncompliance have not been pursued. Third, only a few member countries have translated the rules of the SGP into operationally enforceable targets. In response to Europe's current debt crisis and in an effort to reform the SGP rules, most members of the EU have agreed to a new fiscal pact to prevent member countries from pushing up their debt levels. Among its various provisions, the pact includes fiscal targets with enforcement mechanisms that are purported to be stronger than recent versions. Although the pact was agreed to and signed by officials of most EU countries, it must still be officially ratified by 12 euro zone members before going into effect. Even if ratification occurs, whether member states will comply with the agreement and enforce it effectively remains to be seen. Although the SGP rules have not provided the budgetary discipline that was originally envisioned, some countries have successfully instituted national rules to achieve fiscal sustainability (in some cases as a way to meet the SGP targets). For example, in the mid-1990s, a fiscal crisis in Sweden led the government there to adopt a new fiscal policy framework, which included two targets at the national level: multiple years of expenditure ceilings, and surplus targets covering the general government sector over an economic cycle.[13] Some observers conclude that the ceilings have helped Sweden maintain stable finances.[14] They attribute the nation's favorable budgetary outcomes in part to support for the fiscal framework by the major political parties. In fact, the expenditure ceilings and surplus targets are based neither in legislation nor in a constitution; the political commitment itself acts as the binding force. There are no explicit sanctions for breaching the framework, but policymakers appear to believe that a violation would come at a significant political cost. The ceilings and targets are highly transparent: On several occasions, when fiscal monitors reported that the framework was threatened, that information was published by the media, and corrective actions by the government followed.

End Notes

[1] CBO discussed several alternative tax and spending policies, including the ones reflected in the alternative fiscal scenario, in *An Update to the Budget and Economic Outlook: Fiscal Years 2012 to 2022* (August 2012), pp. 21–23.

[2] Discretionary spending is spending that is controlled through the Congress's annual appropriation process. Mandatory spending is not controlled through that process; rather, it stems from funding provided in other types of legislation or from eligibility criteria and benefit or payment rules set in law.

[3] See Congressional Budget Office, *The 2012 Long-Term Budget Outlook* (June 2012).

[4] For more details about how CBO calculated that difference in growth rates during the past 25 years, see Congressional Budget Office, *The 2012 Long-Term Budget Outlook* (June 2012), p. 53. Potential GDP is the level of GDP that corresponds to a high rate of use of labor and capital.

[5] he ACA refers to the Patient Protection and Affordable Care Act and the health care provisions of the Health Care and Education Reconciliation Act of 2010.

[6] The 40-year average covers a period of diverse economic and fiscal activity and is the benchmark that CBO generally uses when describing budgetary trends. However, other time periods can also provide valid benchmarks.

[7] CBO and the staff of the Joint Committee on Taxation estimate that the provisions of the Affordable Care Act that expand health insurance coverage will have a net cost equal to 0.6 percent of GDP in 2020—the result of an increase of 1.0 percent of GDP in outlays for Medicaid, the Children's Health Insurance Program, and subsidies offered through new health insurance exchanges and related spending, partly offset by an increase of 0.3 percent of GDP in revenues. Under the ACA, reductions in other federal spending and other increases in revenues will slightly more than offset the net cost of the coverage provisions, yielding a net reduction in the deficit, according to CBO's estimates.

[8] Defense spending accounts for about two-fifths of the outlays for that category. Over the past four decades, outlays for defense have averaged 4.7 percent of GDP (they declined from 6.7 percent of GDP in 1972 to 3.0 percent between 1999 and 2001 and then rose to a peak of 4.8 percent in 2010). Under the alternative fiscal scenario, the caps on funding set by the Budget Control Act (excluding the automatic spending reductions scheduled to occur in January) would cause defense spending to grow more slowly than the economy, leaving total outlays for defense at 3.3 percent of GDP in 2020, CBO projects.

[9] For the 40 years between 1968 and 2007 (a period that excludes the effects of the recent recession), total outlays averaged 20.6 percent of GDP.

[10] Over the 40-year period ending in 2007 (which excludes the effects of the recent recession), total revenues averaged 18.2 percent of GDP.

[11] For more details, see Congressional Budget Office, *Federal Debt and the Risk of a Fiscal Crisis* (July 2010).

[12] In CBO's August 2012 baseline, the deficit is projected to total 0.6 percent of GDP in 2020, and debt held by the public is on a downward trajectory.

[13] See Congressional Budget Office, *Reducing the Deficit: Spending and Revenue Options* (March 2011).

[14] CBO and JCT have estimated that repealing all of the provisions of the ACA would increase the deficit in 2020 by $25 billion. See Congressional Budget Office, letter to the Honorable John Boehner providing an estimate for H.R. 6079, the Repeal of Obamacare Act (July 24, 2012).

[15] The estimated budgetary effects shown in Table 3 were not calculated relative to the alternative fiscal scenario but rather relative to CBO's baseline projections (generally, the January 2011 baseline, unless otherwise noted). Measuring the options against the alternative fiscal scenario would probably not materially alter the rough magnitude of the estimates.

[16] Of that projected total, about half is for veterans' benefits, the Supplemental Nutrition Assistance Program, Supplemental Security Income, unemployment compensation, child nutrition, and foster care. Nearly one-third is for federal civilian and military retirement benefits, and the remainder is for other mandatory programs. The $700 billion total excludes offsetting receipts, which reduce outlays.

[17] For more information about the provisions of the Budget Control Act, see Congressional Budget Office, *The Budget and Economic Outlook: An Update* (August 2011), Box 1-1, and *An Update to the Budget and Economic Outlook: Fiscal Years 2012 to 2022* (August 2012), Box 1-1.

[18] They would also reduce mandatory spending by about $15 billion in 2020.

[19] Most federal funding for highways (and for certain other ground and air transportation programs) is controlled by obligation limitations and is not subject to the caps on discretionary budget authority.

[20] See Congressional Budget Office, *Potential Costs of Veterans' Health Care* (October 2010).

[21] Under the Budget Control Act, war-related funding is not constrained by the discretionary caps. However, such funding may decline significantly in coming years because U.S. military activities in Iraq have already wound down and operations in Afghanistan are scheduled to follow suit.

[22] This report does not include options related to military procurement because CBO has previously analyzed such options relative to the Department of Defense's 2011 Future Years Defense Program (a plan covering 2012 to 2016) and has not estimated their effects in 2020. Several such options in CBO's March 2011 *Reducing the Deficit* report were estimated to save a total of about $11 billion in 2016 relative to the Defense Department's plan.

[23] For more discussion of tax expenditures, see Congressional Budget Office, *The Budget and Economic Outlook: Fiscal Years 2012 to 2022* (January 2012), Chapter 4.

[24] The options shown in the table are illustrative. They could be combined as part of a comprehensive deficit reduction plan, but the total additional revenues from such a combination would probably differ from the sum of the revenues shown for the individual options, for three reasons. First, some of the options would interact in ways that would cause their total effect to vary from the sum of the individual provisions. Second, the added revenues from the two options that would extend the earlier tax cuts for some or all taxpayers were estimated relative to the policies in the alternative fiscal scenario, whereas the effects of the other provisions in Table 5 were measured relative to the current-law baseline. Third, estimates for the options to extend the tax cuts are based on more recent economic and technical assumptions than estimates for the other options are.

[25] See Congressional Budget Office, *The 2012 Long Term Budget Outlook* (June 2012).

[26] If such changes excluded people who are 55 or older now, they would not affect roughly 60 percent of the baby-boom generation. If policy changes excluded people who will be 55 or older in 2015, they would not affect roughly 75 percent of baby boomers.

[27] For a more detailed discussion of the economic impact of the fiscal tightening set to occur in January, see Congressional Budget Office, *Economic Effects of Policies Contributing to Fiscal Tightening in 2013* (November 2012).

[28] For a more detailed discussion of the economic impact of fiscal policy in the short term, see the statement of Douglas W. Elmendorf, Director, Congressional Budget Office, before the Senate Budget Committee, *Policies for Increasing Economic Growth and Employment in 2012 and 2013* (November 2011); CBO's methods for analyzing such policies are summarized on pages 22–25 of that testimony. For additional information, see Felix Reichling and Charles Whalen, *Assessing the Short-Term Effects on Output of Changes in Federal Fiscal Policies*, CBO Working Paper 2012-08 (May 2012).

[29] Broadening the tax base would have opposing effects on labor supply. On the one hand, reducing taxpayers' after-tax income would tend to cause them to work more to make up for the loss in income. On the other hand, some approaches for broadening the tax base would raise some taxpayers' marginal tax rates—by pushing them into higher tax brackets, for example—which would tend to cause them to work less. Whether the net effect was positive or negative would depend on the details of the policy change.

[30] See the statement of Douglas W. Elmendorf, Director, Congressional Budget Office, before the Joint Select Committee on Deficit Reduction, *Confronting the Nation's Fiscal Policy*

Challenges (September 2011), pp. 43–47. For a discussion of the methods that CBO uses to assess such effects, see Congressional Budget Office, *The Economic Impact of the President's 2013 Budget* (April 2012), pp. 13–18.

[31] See Congressional Budget Office, *An Update to the Budget and Economic Outlook: Fiscal Years 2012 to 2022* (August 2012), pp. 35–36.

[32] CBO's recent estimates apply to the alternative fiscal scenario as a whole, which includes not only the indexation of the AMT and the extension of the tax provisions originally enacted in the previous decade but other changes in federal taxes and spending. However, the AMT and tax cut provisions represent a larger share of the budgetary effect of the alternative scenario than the other changes do, so the economic impact of those key provisions accounts for most of the economic impact of the alternative scenario as a whole. For an earlier analysis of the effects of those key tax changes alone, see the statement of Douglas W. Elmendorf, Director, Congressional Budget Office, before the Senate Committee on the Budget, *The Economic Outlook and Fiscal Policy Choices* (September 2010).

[33] See Congressional Budget Office, *The Macroeconomic and Budgetary Effects of an Illustrative Policy for Reducing the Federal Budget Deficit* (July 2011). CBO's economic projections for later in this decade and beyond incorporate the favorable long-term impact of the small deficits that will result under current law. Therefore, a reduction in deficits relative to the alternative fiscal scenario would probably not lead CBO to project higher output and income over the medium and long term than are already reflected in the baseline projections.

[34] Lowering the effective marginal tax rate on labor earnings by 5 percentage points would require a larger reduction in statutory tax rates, because some forms of compensation are excluded from taxable income and because some options for broadening the tax base increase people's taxable income and thereby push some of them into higher tax brackets. CBO's reading of the evidence about how the supply of labor responds to changes in tax rates suggests that such a substantial cut in the tax rate would probably increase the labor supply by 2 percent or less; see Congressional Budget Office, *How the Supply of Labor Responds to Changes in Fiscal Policy* (October 2012). Tax restructuring could also boost the capital stock by reducing the effective marginal tax rate on capital income, which would encourage saving, and by generating higher earnings by workers, which would also boost total saving. If those effects together increased the long-term capital stock by an amount comparable to the increase in the labor supply, GDP would rise by 2 percent or less. An increase in GDP of that magnitude would boost federal tax revenues by less than half a percent of GDP.

[35] See Congressional Budget Office, *The Distribution of Household Income and Federal Taxes, 2008 and 2009* (July 2012), p. 3.

End Notes for Appendix

[1] See Andrea Schaechter and others, *Fiscal Rules in Response to the Crisis—Toward the "Next-Generation" Rules, a New Dataset,* Working Paper 12/187 (International Monetary Fund, July 2012), www.imf.org/external/pubs/cat/longres.aspx?sk=26094.0.

[2] Researchers have tried to find a statistical relationship between fiscal rules and fiscal performance. A few studies that looked at policies aimed at significantly reducing a government's annual budget deficits and accumulation of debt showed a positive rela-

tionship between rules and improved fiscal performance (such as a given reduction in debt over a specified period). However, the studies noted that the results were not conclusive and could have been affected by other factors. For instance, a strong political commitment to fiscal discipline, which might be reflected in the introduction of a fiscal rule, could lead to improvements in budgetary performance that would have occurred even without the rule. See Manmohan Kumar and others, *Fiscal Rules—Anchoring Expectations for Sustainable Public Finances,* Policy Paper (International Monetary Fund, December 2009), www.imf.org/external/ pp/longres.aspx?id=4402; Kevin Fletcher and others, *United Kingdom: Selected Issues Paper,* Country Report 10/337 (International Monetary Fund, November 2010), www.imf.org/external/pubs/ cat/longres.aspx?sk=24338.0; and Stephanie Guichard and others, *What Promotes Fiscal Consolidation: OECD Country Experiences,* Economics Department Working Paper 553 (Organisation for Economic Co-operation and Development, May 2007), http:// dx.doi.org/10.1787/180833424370.

[3] See Allen Schick, "The Role of Fiscal Rules in Budgeting," *OECD Journal on Budgeting*, vol. 3, no. 3 (2003), pp. 7–34, www.oecd-ilibrary.org/governance/the-role-of-fiscal-rules-in - budgeting_budget-v3-art14-en.

[4] See George Kopits and Steven A. Symansky, *Fiscal Policy Rules,* Occasional Paper 162 (International Monetary Fund, 1998). The authors conclude that a model fiscal rule should be well-defined, transparent, adequate, consistent, simple, flexible, enforceable, and efficient. However, the authors assert that no rule (or set of rules) combines all of those desirable attributes, partly because some of the attributes inevitably involve trade-offs with others.

[5] Nearly all U.S. state governments also have some form of balanced budget requirement. Those requirements are usually statutory or constitutional in nature; they range from requiring the governor to submit a balanced operating budget to mandating that the governor sign a balanced budget. Such state-level fiscal rules are beyond the scope of this report. For more discussion, see National Conference of State Legislatures, *State Balanced Budget Provisions*, NCSL Fiscal Brief (October 2010), www.ncsl.org/issues-research/ budget/state-balanced-budget-requirements-provisions-and.aspx.

[6] For additional discussion, see the statement of Robert D. Reischauer, Director, Congressional Budget Office, before the Subcommittee on Legislation and National Security of the House Committee on Government Operations, *Budget Enforcement Act* (May 13, 1993).

[7] That deal comprised two laws: the Balanced Budget Act of 1997 and the Taxpayer Relief Act of 1997.

[8] For further discussion, see Congressional Budget Office, *The Budget and Economic Outlook: Fiscal Years 2004–2013* (January 2003), Appendix A; and Allen Schick, "The Role of Fiscal Rules in Budgeting," *OECD Journal on Budgeting,* vol. 3, no. 3 (2003), pp. 7–34, www.oecd-ilibrary.org/governance/the-role-of-fiscal -rules-in-budgeting_budget-v3-art14-en.

[9] "Gross debt" in the European context differs from the measure used in the United States. For European countries, according to definitions used by the IMF and the Organisation for Economic Co-operation and Development, gross debt consists of total financial liabilities for all levels of government (central, state, and local). In the United States, by contrast, gross federal debt consists of debt issued by the federal government to the public as well as debt issued by the Treasury to other federal accounts (intragovernmental debt); it does not include the financial liabilities of state or local governments.

[10] Euro zone membership consisted of 12 countries originally and grew to 17 countries in the late 2000s. Many countries that became members did not in fact meet all of the conditions for

entry into the euro zone. However, the rules stipulated that if countries were approaching the specified levels of each condition at a satisfactory pace, they could be considered to have satisfied the condition.

[11] See Anke Weber, *Stock-Flow Adjustments and Fiscal Transparency: A Cross-Country Comparison*, Working Paper 12/39 (International Monetary Fund, January 2012).

[12] See Ludger Schuknecht and others, *The Stability and Growth Pact: Crisis and Reform*, Occasional Paper 129 (European Central Bank, September 2011), www.ecb.int/pub /scientific/ops/date/html/ opsall.en.html.

[13] See Urban Hansson Brusewitz and Yngve Lindh, "Expenditure Ceilings and Fiscal Policy: Swedish Experiences," in Banca d'Italia, *Public Expenditure* (2005), pp. 667–682.

[14] See, for example, Gösta Ljungman, *Expenditure Ceilings—A Survey,* Working Paper 08/282 (International Monetary Fund, December 2008).

In: Federal Deficit Reduction
Editors: Carl Frankel and Dan Iglehart ISBN: 978-1-62417-779-8

Chapter 2

CONFRONTING THE NATION'S FISCAL POLICY CHALLENGES. STATEMENT OF DOUGLAS W. ELMENDORF, DIRECTOR, CONGRESSIONAL BUDGET OFFICE. HEARING ON "THE HISTORY AND DRIVERS OF OUR NATION'S DEBT AND ITS THREATS"*

Senator Murray, Congressman Hensarling, and Members of the Committee, thank you for the invitation to testify about the outlook for the economy and the budget and about the Congressional Budget Office's (CBO's) analysis of the fiscal policy choices facing this Committee and the Congress.

SUMMARY

The federal government is confronting significant and fundamental budgetary challenges. If current policies are continued in coming years, the aging of the population and the rising cost of health care will boost federal spending, as a share of the economy, well above the amount of revenues that the federal government has collected in the past. As a result, putting the federal budget on a sustainable path will require significant

---

* This is an edited, reformatted and augmented version of statement given on November 13, 2011 before the Joint Select Committee on Deficit Reduction.

changes in spending policies, tax policies, or both. The task of addressing those formidable challenges is complicated by the weakness of the economy and the large numbers of unemployed workers, empty houses, and underused factories and offices. Changes that might be made to federal spending or tax policies could have a substantial impact on the pace of economic recovery during the next few years as well as on the nation's output and people's income over the longer term.

The Economic Outlook

The financial crisis and recession have cast a long shadow on the U.S. economy. Although output began to expand again two years ago, the pace of the recovery has been slow, and the economy remains in a severe slump. CBO expects that the economic recovery will continue but that output will stay well below the economy's potential output—an amount that corresponds to a high rate of use of labor and capital—for several years. CBO published its most recent economic forecast in August; that forecast was initially completed in early July and was updated in August only to reflect the policy changes enacted in the Budget Control Act. Incoming data and other developments since early July, as well as the latest *Blue Chip* consensus forecast, suggest that economic growth for the remainder of this year and next is likely to be weaker than the agency anticipated—with growth in the vicinity of 11/2 percent this year and around 21/2 percent next year.[1]

With output growing at that modest rate, CBO expects employment to expand very slowly during the rest of this year and next year, leaving the unemployment rate close to 9 percent through the end of 2012. Weakness in the demand for goods and services is the principal restraint on hiring, but structural impediments in the labor market— such as a mismatch between the requirements of existing job openings and the characteristics of job seekers—appear to be hindering hiring as well.

If economic growth occurs at the slow pace that CBO anticipates, a large portion of the economic and human costs of the recession and slow recovery remains ahead. In mid-2011, according to the agency's estimates, the economy was only about halfway through the cumulative shortfall in output relative to its potential level that will result from the recession and the weak recovery. Between late 2007 and mid-2011, the cumulative difference between gross domestic product (GDP) and estimated potential GDP amounted to roughly $21/2 trillion; by the time the nation's output rises back to its potential level, probably several years from now, the cumulative shortfall is expected to equal about $5 trillion. Not only are the costs associated with the output gap immense, but they are also borne unevenly, falling disproportionately on people who lose their jobs, who are displaced from their homes, or who own businesses that fail.

The economic outlook remains highly uncertain, however. The recent recession was unusual compared with previous ones in terms of its causes, depth, and duration. As a result, the recovery has had unusual features that have been hard to predict, and the path of the economy in coming years is also likely to be surprising in various ways. Many developments, such as changes in the degree to which households want to further reduce their debt burdens or the adoption of fiscal policies that differ from current law, could cause economic outcomes to differ substantially, in one direction or the other, from those CBO has projected.

The Budget Outlook

If the recovery continues as CBO expects, and if tax and spending policies unfold as specified in current law, deficits will drop markedly as a share of GDP over the next few years. Under CBO's baseline projections, which generally reflect the assumption that current law will not change, deficits fall to 6.2 percent of GDP in 2012 and to 3.2 percent in 2013, and then fluctuate within a range of 1.0 percent to 1.6 percent of GDP from 2014 through 2021. In that scenario, cumulative deficits over the coming decade will total $3.5 trillion, and by 2021, debt held by the public will equal 61 percent of GDP—well above the annual average of 37 percent recorded between 1971 and 2010. (The weaker economy that CBO now anticipates for the remainder of this year and next would imply, all else being equal, a slightly larger federal deficit during that period.)

CBO's baseline projections incorporate the assumption that current law remains in place so they can serve as a benchmark for policymakers to use in considering possible changes to the law. But those baseline projections understate the budgetary challenges facing the federal government because changes in policy that will take effect under current law will produce a federal tax system and spending for some federal programs that differ noticeably from what people have become accustomed to. Specifically, CBO's baseline projections include the following policies specified in current law:

- Provisions of the Tax Relief, Unemployment Insurance Reauthorization, and Job Creation Act of 2010 (Public Law 111-312, referred to in this testimony as the 2010 tax act) that reduced the payroll tax for one year and limited the reach of the alternative minimum tax (AMT) for two years are set to expire on December 31, 2011.
- Several other key provisions of the 2010 tax act—including the extension of lower tax rates and expanded credits and deductions originally enacted in the Economic Growth and Tax Relief Reconciliation Act of 2001, the Jobs and Growth Tax Relief Reconciliation Act of 2003, and the American Recovery and Reinvestment Act (ARRA, P.L. 111-5)—are set to expire on December 31, 2012.
- Medicare's payments for physicians' services are scheduled to be reduced by nearly 30 percent after December 31, 2011.
- Discretionary appropriations between 2012 and 2021 will be subject to statutory caps set in the Budget Control Act of 2011 (P.L. 112-25) that will reduce discretionary spending in real (inflation-adjusted) terms over time.
- Additional budgetary savings of more than $1 trillion required by the Budget Control Act will occur as a result of legislation produced by this Committee or, if lawmakers fail to enact such legislation, by means of automatic cuts in spending that will then be triggered.

Changing provisions of current law so as to maintain major policies that are in effect now would produce markedly different budgetary outcomes. For example, if most of the provisions in the 2010 tax act were extended, if the AMT was indexed for inflation, and if Medicare's payment rates for physicians' services were held constant, then cumulative deficits over the coming decade would total $8.5 trillion, and debt held by the public would reach 82 percent of GDP by the end of 2021, higher than in any year since 1948.

Beyond the coming decade, the fiscal outlook worsens, as the aging of the population and the rising costs of health care exert significant and increasing pressure on the budget under current law. When CBO issued its most recent long-term projections in June 2011, debt held by the public was projected to reach 84 percent of GDP in 2035 under an extension of current law. In those projections, rising federal spending relative to GDP kept debt high even though federal revenues reached significantly larger percentages of GDP than ever seen before in the United States. The agency also examined an alternative scenario in which the tax provisions enacted since 2001 that were extended most recently in 2010 were assumed to be extended, the reach of the AMT was assumed to be restrained to stay close to its historical extent, and tax law was assumed to evolve over the long term so that revenues remained near their historical average of 18 percent of GDP. CBO projected in June that, under that alternative scenario, revenues would increase much more slowly than spending, and debt held by the public would balloon to nearly 190 percent of GDP by 2035.

Although new long-term projections reflecting the latest 10-year projections would differ, the amounts of federal borrowing that would be required under those policy assumptions clearly would be unsustainable. Interest payments on that debt would rise dramatically relative to the size of the tax base that would be available for generating revenues to cover those payments, consuming an ever-growing share of the federal budget. Even before the interest burden became unsupportable, a fiscal crisis could arise if participants in financial markets lost confidence in the government's ability to manage its budget and became unwilling to lend to the government at affordable rates. Thus, under current policies, the federal budget is quickly heading into territory that is unfamiliar to the United States and to most other developed countries as well.

Fiscal Policy Choices

The budgetary and economic challenges facing the nation present policymakers with difficult choices about fiscal policy. As this Committee considers its charge to recommend policies that would reduce future budget deficits, its key choices fall into three broad categories:

- How much deficit reduction should be accomplished?
- How quickly should deficit reduction be implemented?
- What forms should deficit reduction take?

The Magnitude of Deficit Reduction

There is no commonly agreed upon level of federal debt that is sustainable or optimal. Under CBO's current-law baseline, which incorporates $1.2 trillion in expected deficit reduction related to this Committee's work, as well as significant increases in tax revenues relative to GDP, debt held by the public is projected to fall from 67 percent of GDP at the end of 2011 to 61 percent by 2021. However, stabilizing the debt at that level would leave it larger than in any year between 1953 and 2009.

Lawmakers might determine that debt should be reduced to amounts lower than those shown in CBO's baseline—in order to reduce the burden of debt on the economy, relieve some of the long-term pressures on the budget, diminish the risk of a fiscal crisis, and enhance the government's flexibility to respond to unanticipated developments. Accomplishing that objective would require larger amounts of deficit reduction. If, for example, this Committee chose to make recommendations that would lower debt held by the public in 2021 to 50 percent of GDP, roughly the level recorded in the mid-1990s, it would need to propose changes in policies—relative to those embodied in current law, which underlie CBO's baseline projections—that reduced deficits by a total of about $3.8 trillion over the coming decade.

Furthermore, lawmakers might decide that some of the current policies that are scheduled to expire under current law should be continued. In that case, achieving a particular level of debt could require much larger amounts of deficit reduction through other changes in policy. For example, if most of the provisions in the 2010 tax act were extended, if the AMT was indexed for inflation, and if Medicare's payment rates for physicians' services were held constant, then reducing debt held by the public in 2021 to the 61 percent of GDP projected under current law would require other changes in policy to reduce deficits over the next 10 years by a total of $6.2 trillion, rather than the $1.2 trillion in deficit reduction that this Committee would have to accomplish to avoid the automatic budget cuts required by the Budget Control Act.

The Timing of Deficit Reduction

Policymakers face difficult trade-offs in decisions about how quickly to implement policies to reduce budget deficits. On the one hand, cutting spending or increasing taxes slowly would lead to a greater accumulation of government debt and might raise doubts about whether the longer-term deficit reductions would ultimately take effect. On the other hand, implementing spending cuts or tax increases abruptly would give families, businesses, and state and local governments little time to plan and adjust. In addition, and particularly important given the current state of the economy, immediate spending cuts or tax increases would represent an added drag on the weak economic expansion.

However, credible steps to narrow budget deficits over the longer term would tend to boost output and employment in the next few years by holding down interest rates and by reducing uncertainty and enhancing business and consumer confidence. Therefore, the near-term economic effects of deficit reduction would depend on the balance between changes in spending and taxes that take effect quickly and those that take effect gradually. According to CBO's analysis, credible policy changes that would substantially reduce deficits later in the coming decade and over the long term—without immediate cuts in spending or increases in taxes—would both support the economic expansion in the next few years and strengthen the economy over the longer term.

There is no inherent contradiction between using fiscal policy to support the economy today, while the unemployment rate is high and many factories and offices are underused, and imposing fiscal restraint several years from now, when output and employment will probably be close to their potential. If policymakers wanted to achieve both a short-term economic boost and medium-term and long-term fiscal sustainability, a combination of policies would be required: changes in taxes and spending that would widen the deficit now but reduce it later in the decade. Such an approach would work best if the future policy changes were sufficiently specific and widely supported so that households, businesses, state and local governments, and participants in the financial markets believed that the future fiscal restraint would truly take effect.

The Composition of Deficit Reduction

As policymakers consider the composition of policy changes to be used to reduce budget deficits, many factors may play a role. The amount and composition of federal spending and revenues affect the total amount and types of output that are produced and consumed in the country, the distribution of those material resources among various segments of society, and people's well-being in a variety of ways.

In considering the challenge of putting fiscal policy on a sustainable path, many observers have wondered whether it is possible to return to policies regarding federal spending and revenues that, in earlier years, usually generated deficits that were small relative to GDP and kept the amount of debt held by the public to between about one-quarter and one-half of GDP. Unfortunately, however, the past combination of policies cannot be repeated when it comes to the federal budget: The aging of the population and rising costs for health care have changed the backdrop for federal budget policy in a fundamental way.

Under current law, spending on Social Security and the major health care programs— Medicare, Medicaid, the Children's Health Insurance Program, and insurance subsidies to be provided through exchanges in coming years—is projected to be much higher than has historically been the case, reaching 12.2 percent of GDP in 2021, compared with 10.4 percent of GDP in 2011 and an average of 7.2 percent of GDP during the past 40 years. Most of that spending goes to benefits for people over age 65, with smaller shares for blind and disabled people and for nonelderly able-bodied people.

In contrast, under current law, all spending apart from that for Social Security, the major health care programs, and interest payments on the debt is projected to decline noticeably as a share of the economy. That broad collection of programs includes defense (the largest single piece), the Supplemental Nutrition Assistance Program (formerly known as Food Stamps), unemployment compensation, other income-security programs, veterans' benefits, federal civilian and military retirement benefits, transportation, health research, education and training, and other programs. Such spending has averaged 11.5 percent of GDP during the past 40 years and totals 12.0 percent in 2011. Expected improvement in the economy and the caps on discretionary spending instituted in the Budget Control Act are projected to reduce such spending to 7.7 percent of GDP in 2021, the lowest level as a share of GDP in the past 40 years.

Thus, according to CBO's projections under current law, even with the new constraints on discretionary spending, federal spending excluding net interest will grow to 19.9 percent of GDP in 2021—compared with the 40-year average of 18.6 percent. And the composition of that spending will be noticeably different from what the nation has experienced in recent decades: Spending for Social Security and the major health care programs will be much higher, and spending for all other federal programs and activities, except for net interest payments, will be much lower. Alternatively, if the laws governing Social Security and the major health care programs were unchanged, and all other programs were operated in line with their average relationship to the size of the economy during the past 40 years, total federal spending excluding net interest would be much higher in 2021—nearly 24 percent of GDP. That amount exceeds the 40-year average for revenues as a share of GDP by nearly 6 percentage points—even before interest payments on the debt have been included. At the same time, the sharp increase in federal debt and a return to more-normal interest rates will boost the government's net interest costs. They are projected to reach 2.8 percent of GDP in 2021, compared with only 1.5 percent of GDP in 2011 and an average of 2.2 percent of GDP during the past

40 years. What do those numbers imply about the choices that policymakers— and citizens— confront about future policies? Given the aging of the population and the rising costs for health care, attaining a sustainable budget for the federal government will require the United States to deviate from the policies of the past 40 years in at least one of the following ways:

- Raise federal revenues significantly above their average share of GDP;
- Make major changes to the sorts of benefits provided for Americans when they become older; or
- Substantially reduce the role of the rest of the federal government relative to the size of the economy.

The nation cannot continue to sustain the spending programs and policies of the past with the tax revenues it has been accustomed to paying. Citizens will either have to pay more for their government, accept less in government services and benefits, or both.

THE ECONOMIC OUTLOOK

The financial crisis and recession have cast a long shadow on the U.S. economy. Although total output began to expand again two years ago, the pace of the recovery in output and employment has been slow, and the economy remains in a severe slump. Some of the factors that appear to have contributed to economic weakness in the first half of this year—such as a reduction in consumers' purchasing power because of a rise in the price of crude oil—are projected to fade. Nevertheless, CBO expects that the economic recovery will continue to be slow and that real GDP will stay below the economy's potential—a level that corresponds to a high rate of use of labor and capital— for several years (see Figure 1). CBO published its most recent economic forecast in August.[2] The agency initially completed that forecast in early July, and it updated its projections in August to reflect the policy changes enacted in the Budget Control Act of 2011 but no other developments. The news since CBO completed that work suggests that economic growth for the remainder of this year and next is likely to be weaker than the agency anticipated—with growth in the vicinity of 11/2 percent this calendar year (as measured by the change between the fourth quarter of 2010 and the fourth quarter of 2011) and around 21/2 percent next year.[3] (The latest *Blue Chip* consensus forecast for growth in real GDP is 1.3 percent for 2011 and 2.5 percent for 2012.) Those estimates reflect CBO's expectation of continued strong growth in investment by businesses, modest increases in spending by consumers, gains in net exports (exports minus imports), and the beginning of a recovery in new-home construction. With weak economic growth anticipated for the next few years, CBO expects employment to expand very slowly, leaving the unemployment rate close to 9 percent through the end of 2012.

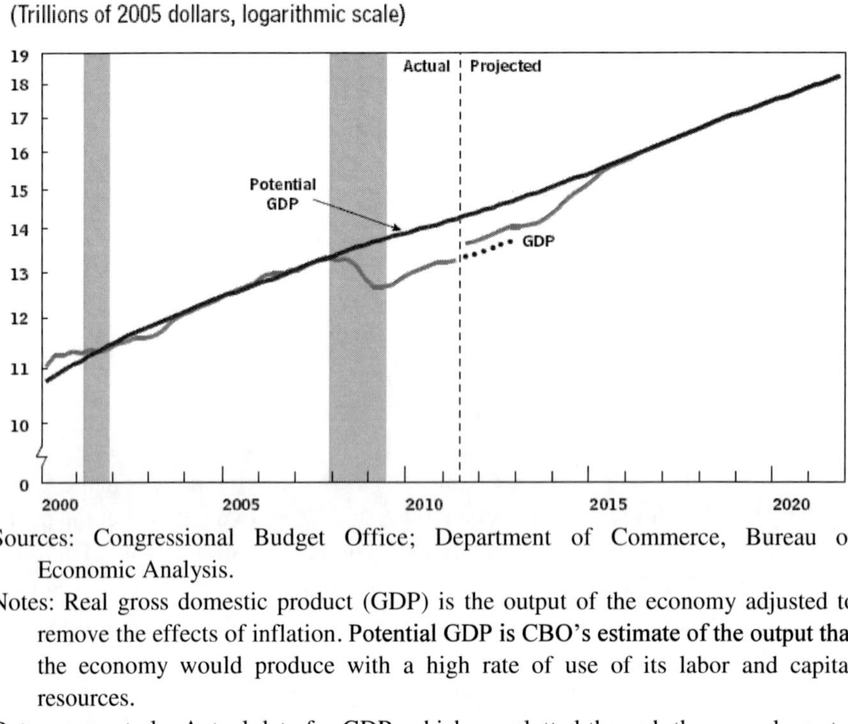

Sources: Congressional Budget Office; Department of Commerce, Bureau of Economic Analysis.

Notes: Real gross domestic product (GDP) is the output of the economy adjusted to remove the effects of inflation. Potential GDP is CBO's estimate of the output that the economy would produce with a high rate of use of its labor and capital resources.

Data are quarterly. Actual data for GDP, which are plotted through the second quarter of 2011, incorporate the July 2011 revisions of the national income and product accounts. The projections of GDP indicated by the solid line are taken from Congressional Budget Office, *The Budget and Economic Outlook: An Update* (August 2011). They are plotted through the fourth quarter of 2021 and are based on data issued before the revisions. The projections of GDP indicated by the dotted line incorporate the effects of the revisions and the news since early July, when the previous forecast was completed; they are plotted through the fourth quarter of 2012.

Figure 1. Real Gross Domestic Product.

The economic outlook remains highly uncertain. The recent recession was unusual compared with previous ones in terms of its causes, depth, and duration. As a result, the recovery has had unusual features that have been hard to predict, and the path of the economy in coming years is also likely to be surprising in various ways. Many developments, such as changes in the degree to which households want to further reduce their debt burdens or the adoption of fiscal policies that differ from current law, could cause economic outcomes to differ substantially, in one direction or the other, from those CBO has projected.

Recent Developments

The period since early July has seen significant financial and economic news that has led many forecasters to lower their projections of near-term growth. In the *Blue Chip* consensus forecast, the probability of a recession by the end of next year now stands at about one-third. Stock prices, as measured by the value of the Standard & Poor's 500 index, fell by more than 12 percent between early July and early September, returning to their level of late 2010. Interest rates on 10-year Treasury notes have dropped by almost a full percentage point since early July from already low levels—mainly because participants in financial markets have sought safer investments because of their concerns about a weaker U.S. economy and potential losses on the sovereign debt of some major euro-zone countries and because the Federal Reserve has signaled its intention to keep short-term interest rates low for an even longer period than many market participants may have expected.

Moreover, employment growth has slowed in the past few months. The total number of jobs increased at an average monthly rate of about 180,000 in the first four months of this year, more than double its average pace in 2010 (see Figure 2). However, employment growth has ebbed again, averaging only 40,000 jobs per month from May through August. Likewise, the unemployment rate fell from 9.8 percent in November 2010 to 8.8 percent in March 2011, but in August, it was back up to 9.1 percent (see Figure 3). Probably reflecting the weak job market and developments such as the declines in stock prices, consumer confidence plunged recently; according to a survey by the University of Michigan, for example, it fell in August to levels last seen during the depths of the recession. The annual revisions to the national income and product accounts (NIPAs) and the first estimate of GDP for the second quarter of 2011, issued by the Commerce Department in late

July, showed that the economy was weaker from 2008 through the first half of 2011 than was previously thought. Real GDP grew at an average annual rate of 0.7 percent in the first half of this year—well below the previous estimate of 1.9 percent that CBO used in constructing its economic forecast in early July. In addition, the revisions indicated that the recession was considerably deeper than previously thought: The total decline in real GDP from its peak in the fourth quarter of 2007 to its trough in the second quarter of 2009 was revised downward from -4.1 percent to -5.1 percent. The figure for subsequent growth of real GDP from the trough of the recession in the second quarter of 2009 through the first quarter of 2011 was also revised downward slightly. With the revisions, real GDP for the first quarter of this year was 1.6 percent lower than previously estimated.

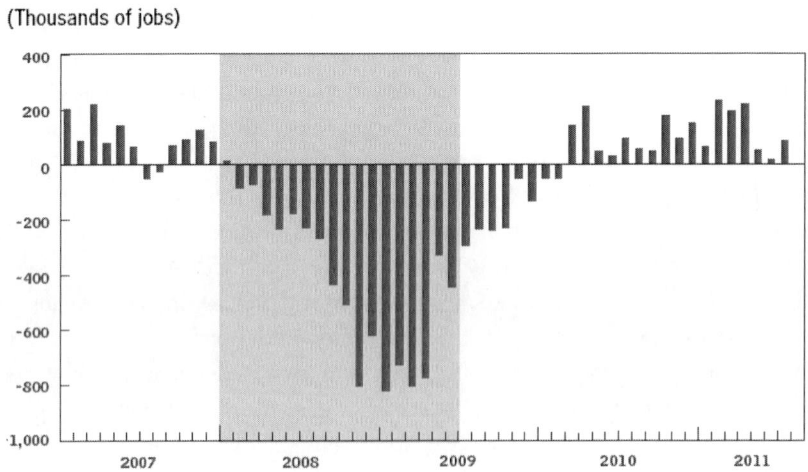

Sources: Congressional Budget Office; Department of Labor, Bureau of Labor Statistics.

Note: Data are monthly and are plotted through August 2011; in that most recent month, net job growth was zero. The data exclude temporary jobs associated with the 2010 census.

Figure 2. Net Job Growth per Month.

Prospects for world economic growth have also deteriorated since early July, which suggests a weaker outlook for U.S. exports. Recent data reveal that growth slowed in major foreign economies during the second quarter of 2011. The annualized growth of real GDP in the euro zone slowed to 0.6 percent in the second quarter from 3.4 percent in the previous quarter, as economic growth in Germany fell sharply. The outlook for growth in China is still bright, but prospects for other Asian economies that rely heavily on exports are softening, and Japan's economy contracted in the second quarter. In addition, the European sovereign debt crisis spread to Spain and Italy, increasing uncertainty and generating volatility in financial markets. The news since early July has not been uniformly negative, though. Oil prices dropped in July and August from their recent highs. In the nonfinancial sector, the data released since early July point to stabilization in both homebuilding and house prices and to a recovery in vehicle sales and production after supply disruptions earlier in the year. In addition, consumer spending appears to have held up, at least through July. Moreover, the revisions to the NIPAs revealed that real gross domestic income, which some consider to be a more accurate indicator of current economic activity than real GDP, grew at a relatively healthy 2.2 percent pace during the first half of 2011, well above the 0.7 percent growth in real GDP.[4]

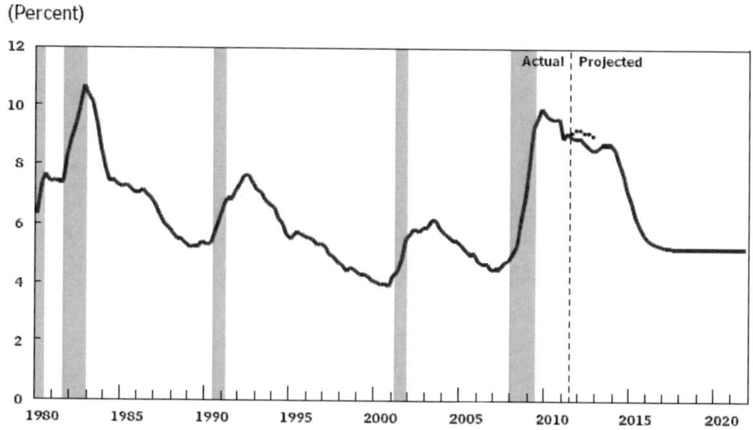

Sources: Congressional Budget Office; Department of Labor, Bureau of Labor Statistics.

Notes: The unemployment rate is a measure of the number of jobless people who are available for work and are actively seeking jobs, expressed as a percentage of the labor force.

Data are quarterly. Actual data are plotted through the second quarter of 2011. The projections indicated by the solid line are taken from Congressional Budget Office, *The Budget and Economic Outlook: An Update* (August 2011) and are plotted through the fourth quarter of 2021. The projections indicated by the dotted line incorporate the effects of the news since early July when the previous forecast was completed; they are plotted through the fourth quarter of 2012.

Figure 3. Unemployment Rate.

The Economic Outlook for 2011 and 2012

CBO expects the pace of economic recovery to pick up a little in the second half of this year but to remain modest for the next few years. Growth slowed and inflation increased in the first half of 2011, in part because of developments that are likely to be temporary, including jumps in energy and food prices and disruptions to the global supply chain caused by the earthquake and nuclear accident in Japan. As the effects of those developments fade, growth in the U.S. economy is likely to rebound a little, driven by continued strength in business investment, modest increases in consumer spending, and expansions in net exports and residential investment. Nevertheless, the pace of growth will probably be restrained for several more years by the lingering effects of the financial crisis and the recession—particularly their impact on households' net worth and indebtedness, on access to credit for riskier borrowers, on the number of vacant homes, and on consumer and business confidence. The growth in GDP that CBO now anticipates—about 11/2 percent this year (as measured by the change between the fourth quarter of 2010 and the fourth quarter of 2011) and around 21/2 percent next year—would be weaker than what CBO forecast in August, when it projected real GDP growth of 2.3 percent in 2011 and 2.7 percent in 2012. Other forecasters have also modified their expectations. For example, between early July and early September, the *Blue Chip* consensus forecast for real GDP growth in 2011 was marked down from 2.6 percent to 1.3 percent. For 2012, the *Blue Chip* forecast was lowered from 3.0 percent to 2.5 percent. With modest growth in output, CBO expects employment to expand very slowly during the rest of this year and next year. Weakness in the demand for goods and services is the principal restraint on hiring, but structural impediments in the labor market— such as a mismatch between the requirements of existing job openings and the characteristics of job seekers (including their skills and geographic location)—appear to be hindering hiring as well. As a result, the unemployment rate is likely to be around 9.0 percent through the fourth quarter of next year. (In CBO's August forecast, the unemployment rate fell to 8.5 percent by the fourth quarter of 2012.) Between early July and early September, the *Blue Chip* consensus similarly raised its forecast for the unemployment rate in the fourth quarter of 2012—from 8.1 percent to 8.7 percent. Inflation increased markedly in the first half of 2011, spurred in large part by a sharp rise in oil prices, but CBO projects that it will diminish in the second half of the year and be low in 2012 (see Figure 4). The increase in oil prices since mid-2010 has been partly reversed, and trading in financial markets points to fairly stable prices for oil and other commodities in the next few years. In addition, the large amount of unused or underemployed resources in the economy will continue to hold down the growth of wages and prices. CBO now projects that the price index for personal consumption expenditures (PCE) will increase by about 21/2 percent this year and by about 11/2 percent next year (as measured by the change from the fourth quarter of the previous year). The "core" version of the PCE price index, which excludes prices for food and energy, is projected to rise by about 13/4 percent in 2011 and by about 11/2 percent in 2012. The consumer price index for all urban consumers and its core version are expected to increase more rapidly than their PCE counterparts, especially in 2011.

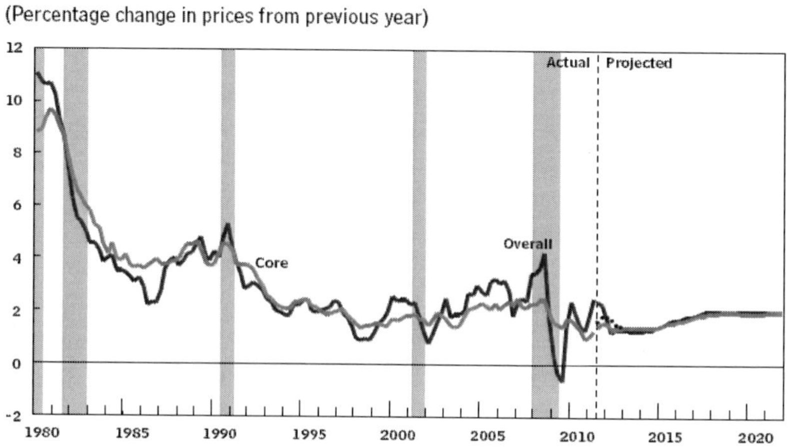

Sources: Congressional Budget Office; Department of Commerce, Bureau of Economic Analysis.

Notes: The overall inflation rate is based on the price index for personal consumption expenditures; the core rate excludes prices for food and energy.

Data are quarterly. Actual data, which are plotted through the second quarter of 2011, incorporate the July 2011 revisions of the national income and product accounts. The projections indicated by the solid lines are taken from Congressional Budget Office, *The Budget and Economic Outlook: An Update* (August 2011). They are plotted through the fourth quarter of 2021 and are based on data issued before the revisions. The projections indicated by the dotted line are for core inflation and incorporate the effects of the revisions and the news since early July, when the previous forecast was completed; they are plotted through the fourth quarter of 2012.

Figure 4. Inflation.

CBO now expects inflation in 2011, as measured by both the PCE price index and the consumer price index, to be higher than it forecast in August because gasoline prices have remained high and inflation in housing rents has been higher than projected; expected higher inflation in rents accounts for CBO's higher inflation forecast in 2012. With modest inflation and slow economic growth, interest rates are likely to remain quite low for the rest of 2011 and 2012. The interest rate on 3-month Treasury bills is likely to remain barely above zero, and as indicated by the financial markets, the rate on 10-year Treasury notes will probably average less than 3.0 percent.

The Output Gap and Its Costs

Economic growth at the rates CBO anticipates would leave a very large and persistent gap between actual output and the agency's estimate of potential output—that is, a large amount of labor and capital resources would be unused for some time. In CBO's August baseline projections, the output gap is about 5 percent of potential GDP at the end of 2011 and does not close fully until the second half of the 2011–2021 projection period.[5]

As a result, a large portion of the economic and human costs of the recession and slow recovery remains ahead. In mid-2011, according to CBO's estimates, the economy was only about halfway through the cumulative shortfall in output relative to its potential level that will result from the recession and the weak recovery. Between late 2007 and mid-2011, the cumulative difference between GDP and estimated potential GDP amounted to roughly $21/2 trillion; by the time the nation's output rises back to its potential level, the cumulative shortfall is expected to equal about $5 trillion.

Not only are the costs associated with the output gap immense, but they are also borne unevenly. Those costs fall disproportionately on people who lose their jobs, who are displaced from their homes, or who own businesses that fail. In the first quarter of 2011, for example, the recession and weak recovery led to a shortfall of about 10 million jobs relative to the number that would have existed had the recession not occurred and had job growth matched the average rate in the previous business cycle. And the unemployment rate is projected to remain well above CBO's estimate of the natural rate of unemployment for several years.[6] Even among workers who find a new job, experience suggests that many will end up with lower earnings, not only in the short term but for many years to come.[7]

Uncertainty in the Economic Outlook

Economic forecasts are always subject to a considerable degree of uncertainty, but the uncertainty surrounding the economic outlook is especially great because the present business cycle has been unusual in a variety of ways. CBO constructs its economic forecasts to lie in the middle of the distribution of possible future outcomes for the economy under an assumption that current law remains unchanged. Actual outcomes will undoubtedly differ from what CBO has projected in at least some respects. Key areas of uncertainty in the economic outlook include the following factors:

- The degree to which households want to further reduce their debt burdens, The pace at which firms hire and invest,
- The timing and magnitude of a recovery in house prices,
- The evolution in people's confidence about their future economic gains, Changes in stock prices and long-term interest rates,
- The resolution of concerns that some European governments may default on their debts, and
- The path of U.S. fiscal policy.

Different outcomes for those factors could combine to have quite divergent effects: from boosting the growth of the U.S. economy significantly to causing a new recession, or producing some result in between.

On the upside, the economy could grow considerably faster than CBO anticipates if the forces that have restrained the recovery fade more rapidly than the agency anticipates. The most important of those forces are the ones holding down consumer spending, including weak growth in employment and income as well as the loss of wealth from declines in house and stock prices. If wages and salaries grew faster than CBO projects—because of a shift in national income toward employee compensation and away from profits, for example—then they could support stronger consumer spending. If that faster growth in compensation was matched by gains in house prices and further easing of constraints on lending, then consumer spending could be buttressed by increased net worth and faster growth in consumer credit. Those conditions could in turn speed up the growth of employment and boost businesses' spending on facilities and equipment, potentially leading to a self-reinforcing cycle of increased spending, hiring, and income.

That favorable chain of events could be bolstered by renewed stability in financial markets or declines in the prices of oil and other commodities. In addition, foreign demand for U.S. goods and services could be greater than CBO expects if fears of negative financial repercussions from default on European sovereign debt proved to be exaggerated and if economic expansion in India, China, and other parts of the developing world ended up being stronger than expected.

However, outcomes that are considerably worse than CBO projects are also possible. The slowing of growth in U.S. output during the first half of 2011 might portend the onset of another recession. Although current economic indicators are not pointing to the kinds of imbalances that have preceded previous recessions, one possible path to a new recession would be a self-reinforcing downward spiral in which reduced hiring led to weaker growth of household income and diminished consumer and business confidence, which in turn led to lower spending by households and businesses and thus less need for workers and less hiring. Stock prices could continue to fall, reducing households' wealth and confidence. In addition, problems in housing and mortgage markets could persist longer than anticipated, which could push down house prices further, prolong problems in the financial system, and further restrain consumer spending and residential construction. Under those conditions, the income and confidence of businesses and households would decline further, and such a cycle of self-reinforcing adjustments could drive the economy into recession again.

Another possible catalyst for a recession is a worsening of the sovereign debt crisis in Europe, leading to more turmoil in international financial markets, potentially spilling over to U.S. financial markets, which have been fragile recently. If that occurred while policymakers in some developing countries were already slowing their economies to counteract inflationary pressures, economic activity worldwide could contract. The problems for the U.S. economy would be compounded if oil prices spiked because of further political unrest or military conflict in oil-producing states that threatened to disrupt the supply of oil. The problems would also be amplified if concerns about large federal deficits and the high current level of federal debt restricted policymakers' ability to use fiscal policy to address the effects of an economic crisis.

THE BUDGET OUTLOOK

In part because of the weak economy and actions the government has taken in response, the budget deficit in fiscal year 2011 will total nearly $1.3

trillion, CBO estimates.[8] At 8.5 percent of GDP, this year's deficit will be the third-largest shortfall in the past 65 years, exceeded only by those in 2009 (at 10.0 percent) and 2010 (at 8.9 percent). As a result, at the end of the current fiscal year (September 30, 2011), debt held by the public will stand at an estimated 67 percent of GDP—the highest level since 1950 and up from 40 percent at the end of fiscal year 2008.

CBO's Budget Projections for 2012 to 2021

During the next several years and over the longer term, the nation faces profound challenges regarding the federal budget. The future paths of federal deficits and debt will depend crucially both on the strength of the economic recovery and on the tax and spending policies pursued by the federal government. In CBO's baseline estimates, which generally reflect the assumption that current law will not change, deficits drop markedly as a share of GDP over the next few years.[9] Under current law, CBO projects, the deficit will fall to 6.2 percent of GDP in 2012 and to 3.2 percent in 2013, and then will fluctuate within a range of 1.0 percent to 1.6 percent of GDP from 2014 through 2021 (see Table 1). (The weaker economy that CBO now anticipates for the remainder of this year and next would imply, all else being equal, a slightly larger federal deficit during that period.) In that scenario, deficits will total $3.5 trillion between 2012 and 2021, and by 2021, debt held by the public will equal 61 percent of GDP—well above the annual average of 37 percent recorded between 1971 and 2010.

However, the budgetary challenges facing the federal government are not fully reflected in CBO's baseline projections because current law provides for substantial changes to tax and spending policies in coming years. If those changes did not occur and current policies were continued instead, much larger deficits and much greater debt would result (see Figure 5). Specifically, current law includes the following features whose modification or elimination could significantly increase future deficits and debt:

- Provisions of the Tax Relief, Unemployment Insurance Reauthorization, and Job Creation Act of 2010 that reduced the payroll tax for one year and limited the reach of the alternative minimum tax for two years are set to expire on December 31, 2011.

Table 1. CBO's Baseline Budget Outlook

	Actual, 2010	2011	2012	2013	2014	2015	2016	2017	2018	2019	2020	2021	Total 2012-2016	Total 2012-2021
	In Billions of Dollars													
Projection Excluding Effects of Provisions Related to the Joint Select Committee on Deficit Reduction														
Revenues	2,163	2,314	2,635	3,069	3,423	3,655	3,847	4,087	4,286	4,508	4,731	4,969	16,640	39,221
Outlays	3,456	3,597	3,609	3,692	3,803	3,988	4,249	4,449	4,635	4,913	5,161	5,409	19,340	43,908
Deficit	-1,294	-1,284	-973	-623	-380	-322	-402	-362	-349	-405	-430	-440	-2,701	-4,687
Effects of Provisions Related to the Joint Select Committee on Deficit Reduction[a]	0	0	0	113	115	118	124	132	139	146	154	161	469	1,200
Total Deficit	**-1,294**	**-1,284**	**-973**	**-510**	**-265**	**-205**	**-278**	**-231**	**-211**	**-259**	**-277**	**-279**	**-2,232**	**-3,487**
Debt Held by the Public at the End of the Year	9,019	10,164	11,153	11,773	12,148	12,453	12,840	13,169	13,473	13,820	14,181	14,541	n.a.	n.a.

	As a Percentage of Gross Domestic Product													
Projection Excluding Effects of Provisions Related to the Joint Select Committee on Deficit Reduction														
Revenues	14.9	15.3	16.8	19.0	20.2	20.2	20.1	20.4	20.5	20.6	20.7	20.9	19.3	20.0
Outlays	23.8	23.8	23.0	22.8	22.4	22.0	22.2	22.2	22.1	22.4	22.6	22.7	22.5	22.4
Deficit	-8.9	-8.5	-6.2	-3.9	-2.2	-1.3	-2.1	-1.8	-1.7	-1.8	-1.9	-1.8	-3.1	-2.4
Effects of Provisions Related to the Joint Select Committee on Deficit Reduction[a]	0	0	0	0.7	0.7	0.5	0.6	0.7	0.7	0.7	0.7	0.7	0.5	0.6
Total Deficit	**-8.9**	**-8.5**	**-6.2**	**-3.2**	**-1.6**	**-1.1**	**-1.5**	**-1.2**	**-1.0**	**-1.2**	**-1.2**	**-1.2**	**-2.6**	**-1.8**
Debt Held by the Public at the End of the Year	62.1	67.3	71.2	72.8	71.6	68.7	67.2	65.8	64.3	63.1	62.0	61.0	n.a.	n.a.

Source: Congressional Budget Office.

Notes: The Budget Control Act of 2011 (Public Law 112-25) created the Joint Select Committee on Deficit Reduction to propose further deficit reduction totaling at least $1.5 trillion over 10 years. The act also specified automatic procedures for reducing spending by as much as $1.2 trillion if legislation originating with the new deficit reduction committee does not achieve savings of at least $1.2 trillion. CBO has incorporated that amount of deficit reduction (which includes savings in debt-service costs) in its baseline but has no basis for allocating that amount between revenues and outlays. Policy changes were allocated evenly across the 2013–2021 period; the incremental increase in the annual effects results from the compounding of debt-service savings.

n.a. = not applicable.

a. Includes effects on debt service.

- Several other key provisions of the 2010 tax act—including the extension of lower tax rates and expanded credits and deductions originally enacted in the Economic Growth and Tax Relief Reconciliation Act of 2001, the Jobs and Growth Tax Relief Reconciliation Act of 2003, and the American Recovery and Reinvestment Act are set to expire on December 31, 2012.
- Medicare's payments for physicians' services are scheduled to be reduced by nearly 30 percent after December 31, 2011.
- Discretionary appropriations between 2012 and 2021 will be subject to statutory caps set in the Budget Control Act of 2011. If adhered to, those caps will reduce discretionary outlays by about 5 percent in real terms over the 2012–2021 period relative to spending in 2011, CBO estimates.[10]
- Additional budgetary savings of more than $1 trillion required by the Budget Control Act will occur as a result of legislation produced by this Committee or, if lawmakers fail to enact such legislation, by means of automatic cuts in spending that will then be triggered.

Under an assumption that those provisions of current law all remain in place, CBO projects that revenues will rise sharply—from 15.3 percent of GDP in 2011 to 20.2 percent in 2014 and to 20.9 percent by 2021. Outlays, by contrast, are projected to decrease as a percentage of GDP over the next few years, falling from 23.8 percent of GDP in 2011 to a low of 22.0 percent of GDP in 2015, before increasing again to 22.7 percent by 2021. (Those projections of revenues and outlays exclude the effects of changes that might occur as a result of provisions of the Budget Control Act related to the deficit reduction committee because CBO cannot predict what those changes might be.) By comparison, during the past 40 years, revenues have represented 18.0 percent of GDP, on average, and outlays have represented 20.8 percent. Changing provisions of current law so as to maintain major policies that are in effect now would produce markedly different budgetary outcomes. For example, if most of the provisions in the 2010 tax act were extended (rather than allowed to expire on December 31, 2012) and if the AMT was indexed for inflation, CBO projects that annual revenues would average 18 percent of GDP from 2012 through 2021, rather than the 20 percent shown in the baseline projections.[11] If Medicare's payment rates for physicians' services also were held constant, then deficits from 2012 through 2021 would average 4.3 percent of GDP, compared with the 1.8 percent in the baseline.

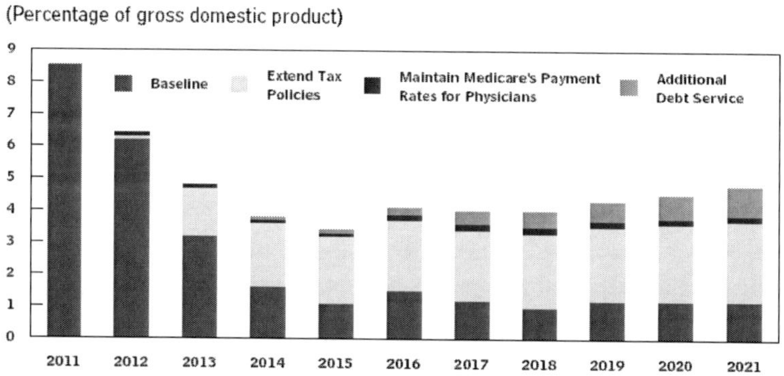

Note: "Extend Tax Policies" reflects the following policy assumptions: Most of the provisions in the 2010 tax act that were originally enacted in 2001, 2003, 2009, and 2010 are extended (instead of being allowed to expire on December 31, 2012, as scheduled), and the alternative minimum tax is indexed for inflation. "Maintain Medicare's Payment Rates for Physicians" involves preventing the nearly 30 percent reduction in Medicare's payment rates for physicians' services that is scheduled to take effect at the end of 2011. "Additional Debt Service" is the amount of interest payments on the additional debt issued to the public that would result from the continuation of the specified policies.

Figure 5. Deficits in CBO's Baseline and Assuming a Continuation of Certain Policies.

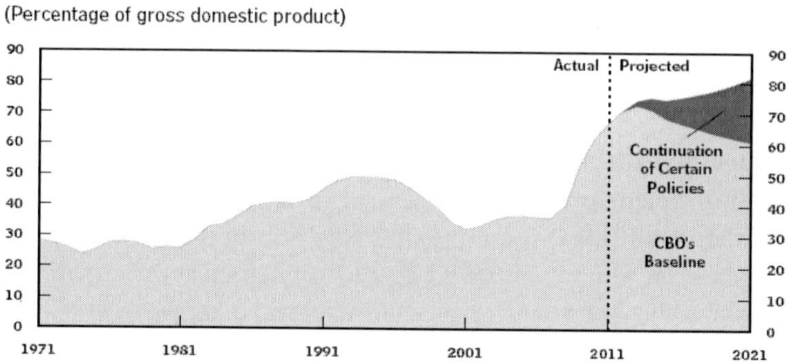

Source: Congressional Budget Office.

Note: The projected debt with the continuation of certain policies is based on several assumptions: first, that most of the provisions of the Tax Relief, Unemployment Insurance Reauthorization, and Job Creation Act of 2010 (Public Law 111-312) that originally were enacted in 2001, 2003, 2009, and 2010 do not expire on December 31, 2012, but instead continue; second, that the alternative minimum tax is indexed for inflation after 2011; and third, that Medicare's payment rates for physicians are held constant at their 2011 level.

Figure 6. Federal Debt Held by the Public.

With cumulative deficits during that decade of nearly $8.5 trillion under such policies, debt held by the public would reach 82 percent of GDP by the end of 2021, higher than in any year since 1948 (see Figure 6).

The projected deficits reflect the fact that, during the coming decade and over the long term, the aging of the population and rising costs of health care will exert significant and increasing pressure on the budget. The number of people age 65 or older will increase by roughly one-third between 2011 and 2021, causing that segment of the U.S. population to climb from 13 percent to 17 percent of the total; beyond 2021, that share will rise further. In addition, the major health care legislation enacted in 2010 will increase the number of beneficiaries of federal health care programs, and CBO projects that the costs of those programs per beneficiary will continue rising (albeit at different rates because of differences in the laws that govern them). All told, outlays for Social Security, Medicare, and Medicaid—which will account for 44 percent of all federal noninterest spending in 2011—will continue to rise relative to GDP and to consume a growing share of the federal budget.

The Budget Control Act of 2011

CBO's current baseline projections show smaller deficits than the agency estimated earlier this year primarily because of the enactment of the Budget Control Act of 2011.[12] Provisions in that act:

- Establish caps on discretionary funding through 2021;
- Allow certain amounts of additional spending for "program integrity" initiatives aimed at curtailing improper benefit payments;
- Change the Pell Grant and student loan programs;
- Require the House of Representatives and the Senate to vote on a joint resolution proposing a balanced budget amendment to the Constitution;
- Establish a procedure for increasing the debt limit by $400 billion initially and procedures to raise the limit again in two additional steps, for a cumulative increase of between $2.1 trillion and $2.4 trillion;
- Reinstate and modify certain budget process rules;
- Create the Congressional Joint Select Committee on Deficit Reduction to propose further reductions that will amount to at least $1.5 trillion in budgetary savings over 10 years; and

- Establish automatic procedures for reducing spending if legislation originating with the new deficit reduction committee does not achieve savings estimated to total at least $1.2 trillion.

Discretionary Caps

The Budget Control Act imposes caps on appropriations of new discretionary budget authority that start at $1,043 billion in 2012 and reach $1,234 billion in 2021. For 2012 and 2013, separate caps for "security" and "non-security" budget authority will be in effect; from 2014 through 2021, only one cap will apply to total discretionary funding unless automatic spending reductions are triggered (as described below under "Enforcement Procedures").[13]

The law allows for adjustments to the discretionary caps when appropriations are provided for certain purposes. Funding for the wars in Afghanistan and Iraq or similar activities (sometimes called overseas contingency operations) would lead to an increase in the caps, as would other funding designated as an emergency requirement. Furthermore, the law allows for an increase in the caps if additional budget authority is provided for program integrity initiatives aimed at reducing improper benefit payments in the Disability Insurance and Supplemental Security Income programs, Medicare, Medicaid, and the Children's Health Insurance Program. Finally, the caps would be increased if appropriations were provided for disaster relief, but the adjustments would be limited on the basis of historical averages for such funding.

According to CBO's estimates, if appropriations in the next 10 years are equal to the caps on discretionary spending, implementing those caps will reduce budget deficits by $756 billion between 2012 and 2021 (not counting the savings in interest payments that will result from lower outlays), compared with what would occur if discretionary budget authority was allowed to grow at the rate of inflation.

Overall Budgetary Impact of the Act

The law also made changes to education programs that will reduce mandatory outlays over the 2012–2021 period by $5 billion. The savings in interest on the public debt because of the lower deficits resulting from those changes and the discretionary caps will come to $134 billion, CBO estimates.[14] In addition, CBO's estimate of the budgetary impact of the law, as well as the agency's August baseline projections, include further deficit reduction totaling $1.2 trillion over the 10-year period stemming from legislation originating with the deficit reduction committee or the automatic reductions in spending that will occur in the absence of such legislation. (As discussed on the following page, CBO estimates that enforcement of the act, in the absence of any enacted legislation stemming from the committee's recommendations, would result in net savings of about $1.1 trillion over the coming decade.) The composition of that additional deficit reduction over time and across budget categories will depend on the specific provisions of any legislation stemming from the committee's proposals and the extent of any automatic reductions that would be triggered. Overall, CBO's baseline projections incorporate $2.1 trillion in deficit reduction over the 2012–2021 period stemming from the act.

Enforcement Procedures

If legislation originating from this Committee and estimated to produce at least $1.2 trillion in deficit reduction (including an allowance for interest savings) is not enacted by January 15, 2012, automatic procedures for cutting both discretionary and mandatory spending would take effect.[15] The magnitude of those cuts would depend on any shortfall in the estimated effects of such legislation relative to the $1.2 trillion amount.

The automatic reductions—if triggered—would take the form of equal cuts (in dollar terms) in defense and nondefense spending starting in 2013. Those cuts would be achieved by lowering the caps on discretionary budget authority specified in the Budget Control Act and by automatically cancelling budgetary resources (a process known as sequestration) for some programs and activities financed by mandatory spending.[16] The law exempts a significant portion of mandatory spending from sequestration, however. The total savings attributed to the automatic procedures would include lower debt-service costs resulting from those cuts.

CBO has estimated the changes in discretionary and mandatory spending that would occur if the automatic enforcement mechanisms were triggered because no new deficit reduction legislation was enacted. CBO's analysis can only approximate the ultimate results; the Administration's Office of Management and Budget would be responsible for implementing any such automatic reductions on the basis of its own estimates. CBO estimates that, if no legislation originating from this Committee was enacted, the automatic enforcement process specified in the Budget Control Act would produce the following results between 2013 and 2021:

- Reductions ranging from 10.0 percent (in 2013) to 8.5 percent (in 2021) in the caps on new discretionary appropriations for defense programs, yielding total outlay savings of $454 billion.
- Reductions ranging from 7.8 percent (in 2013) to 5.5 percent (in 2021) in the caps on new discretionary appropriations for nondefense programs, resulting in outlay savings of $294 billion.
- Reductions ranging from 10.0 percent (in 2013) to 8.5 percent (in 2021) in mandatory budgetary resources for nonexempt defense programs, generating savings of about $0.1 billion.
- Reductions of 2.0 percent each year in most Medicare spending because of the application of a special rule that applies to that program, producing savings of $123 billion, and reductions ranging from 7.8 percent (in 2013) to 5.5 percent (in 2021) in mandatory budgetary resources for other nonexempt nondefense programs and activities, yielding savings of $47 billion. Thus, savings in nondefense mandatory spending would total $170 billion.
- About $31 billion in outlays stemming from reductions in premiums for Part B of Medicare and other changes in spending that would result from the sequestration actions.
- An estimated reduction of $169 billion in debt-service costs.

In all, those automatic cuts would produce net budgetary savings of about $1.1 trillion over the 2013–2021 period, CBO estimates. That amount is lower than the $1.2 trillion figure for deficit reduction in the Budget Control Act for three reasons. First, because of the lag in timing between appropriations and subsequent expenditures, part of the savings from the automatic cuts in budgetary resources would occur after 2021. Second, CBO expects that some reductions—particularly those related to Medicare—would have other effects that would boost net spending (by the $31 billion mentioned above). Third, CBO estimates that the reduction in debt-service costs would be lower than the amount of such savings stipulated in the Budget Control Act.[17]

The majority of the savings from the automatic spending reductions would stem from further cuts in discretionary spending (beyond those embodied in the new law's caps on discretionary budget authority). CBO expects that about 71 percent of the net savings from the automatic procedures would come from lowering the caps on discretionary appropriations, 13 percent would come from a net reduction in mandatory spending, and 16 percent would result from lower debt-service costs.

Of course, the Budget Control Act could produce outcomes that are very different from the figures outlined above. The Congress could enact legislation originating from this Committee that would produce $1.2 trillion in savings through changes that differ significantly from the automatic reductions that would be required in the absence of such legislation. Or such legislation could yield some savings, but less than $1.2 trillion, so the automatic procedures would have a smaller impact than CBO has estimated here. Alternatively, this Committee could recommend, and the Congress could enact, legislation saving significantly more than $1.2 trillion. (The Budget Control Act states that the Committee's goal is to achieve at least $1.5 trillion in savings over the 2012–2021 period.)[18]

The Long-Term Budget Outlook

Beyond the coming decade, the fiscal outlook worsens. When CBO issued its most recent long-term projections in June 2011, debt held by the public was projected to reach 76 percent of GDP in 2021 under current law.[19] Beyond 2021, under an extension of current law that CBO labeled the "extended-baseline scenario," debt was projected to rise to 84 percent of GDP in 2035. Because CBO's projections based on current law now show that debt held by the public will be declining relative to GDP after 2013 (to 61 percent in 2021), the long-term outlook under current law is a little brighter than it was earlier in the year. Even under the latest projections, however, debt would still be larger relative to GDP in 2021 than in any year between 1953 and 2009. Moreover, although long-term budget projections are highly uncertain, the aging of the population and rising costs for health care would almost certainly push federal spending up sharply relative to GDP after 2021 if current law remained in effect. Federal revenues also would continue to increase relative to GDP after 2021 under current law, reaching significantly higher percentages of GDP than ever seen before in the United States. CBO has not updated its long-term projections to reflect its new 10-year baseline, and the net effect that those trends in outlays and revenues would have on budget deficits beyond 2021 is not clear.

Under certain policy assumptions other than those underlying CBO's baseline, the budget outlook is much bleaker—both for the next 10 years and over the longer term. In CBO's long-term projections issued in June, the agency also examined an "alternative fiscal scenario," which incorporated several changes to current law that are widely expected to occur or that would modify some provisions of law that might be difficult to sustain for a long period. Specifically, the tax provisions enacted since 2001 that were extended most recently in 2010 were assumed to be extended, the reach of the AMT was assumed to be restrained to stay close to its historical extent, and tax law was assumed to evolve over the long term so that revenues remained near their historical average of 18 percent of GDP. CBO projected in June that, under the alternative fiscal scenario, revenues would increase much more slowly than spending, and debt held by the public would balloon to nearly 190 percent of GDP by 2035.

Although new long-term projections reflecting the latest 10-year projections would differ, the amounts of federal borrowing that would be required under those policy assumptions clearly would be unsustainable. Moreover, the projections of federal debt that CBO highlighted in June for the alternative fiscal scenario do not include the harmful effects of rising debt on economic growth and interest rates. If those effects were taken into account, projected debt would increase even more rapidly. Thus, under current policies, the federal budget is quickly heading into territory that is unfamiliar to the United States and to most other developed countries as well.

Fiscal Policy Choices

The budgetary and economic challenges facing the nation present policymakers with difficult choices about fiscal policy. As this Committee considers its charge to recommend policies that would reduce future budget deficits, its key choices fall into three broad categories:

- How much deficit reduction should be accomplished?
- How quickly should deficit reduction be implemented?
- What forms should deficit reduction take?

The Magnitude of Deficit Reduction

There is no commonly agreed upon level of federal debt that is sustainable or optimal. At a minimum, federal debt cannot continually increase as a share of the economy because the interest payments on that debt would then continually grow relative to the size of the tax base that would be available for generating revenues to cover those payments and all of the other activities of the government. Even before the interest burden became unsupportable, a fiscal crisis could arise if participants in financial markets lost confidence in the government's ability to manage its budget and became unwilling to lend to the government at affordable rates.[20]

Under CBO's current-law baseline, which incorporates $1.2 trillion in expected deficit reduction related to this Committee's work, debt held by the public falls from 67 percent of GDP at the end of 2011 to 61 percent by 2021. However, stabilizing the debt at that level relative to GDP would leave it larger than in any year from 1953 through 2009. Moreover, an aging population and rising health care costs will exert significant and increasing pressure on the budget in the years beyond 2021.

Lawmakers might determine that debt should be reduced to amounts lower than those shown in CBO's baseline—in order to reduce the burden of debt on the economy, relieve some of the long-term pressures on the budget, diminish the risk of a fiscal crisis, and enhance the government's flexibility to respond to unanticipated developments. Accomplishing that objective would require larger amounts of deficit reduction. For example, to lower debt held by the public in 2021 to 50 percent of GDP, roughly the same level recorded in the mid-1990s, budget deficits during the next decade would need to be about $2.6 trillion lower than in CBO's baseline. If this Committee aimed to achieve that goal through its own recommendations, it would need to propose changes in policies that would reduce deficits by a total of about $3.8 trillion (including interest savings) over the coming decade.

Furthermore, the current laws that underlie CBO's baseline projections provide for significant changes to tax and spending policies in coming years. Lawmakers might decide that some of those current policies should be continued. In that case, achieving a particular level of debt could require much larger amounts of deficit reduction through other changes in policy.

For example, if most of the provisions in the 2010 tax act were extended, if the AMT was indexed for inflation, and if Medicare's payment rates for physicians' services were held constant, then in the absence of other policy changes, deficits over the next 10 years would total $8.5 trillion—compared with $3.5 trillion in the baseline—and debt held by the public would reach 82 percent of GDP in 2021, well above both the current level and the projected level in 2021 under current law. If lawmakers decided to change the law in order to extend those policies, then reducing debt held by the public in 2021 to the 61 percent of GDP projected under current law would require other changes in policy that reduced deficits over the next 10 years by $5 trillion in addition to the $1.2 trillion in deficit reduction that this Committee would have to accomplish to avoid the automatic budget cuts required by the Budget Control Act. If this Committee aimed to achieve that goal through its own recommendations, it would need to propose changes in policies that reduced deficits (apart from the effects of extending those existing policies) by a total of about $6.2 trillion (including interest savings) over the coming decade. To lower debt held by the public to the 50 percent of GDP seen in the mid-1990s would require significantly larger reductions in deficits. In 2021 alone, the gap between federal revenues and spending if those policies were continued and no other budgetary changes were made would be $1.1 trillion, or 4.7 percent of GDP, CBO projects (see Figure 7). Given CBO's forecast of economic growth and interest rates in that year, the deficit would need to be less than 2.2 percent of GDP to put debt on a downward trajectory relative to GDP. Relative to the benchmark of continuing those policies, reaching that objective would require a reduction in the deficit of roughly 2.5 percent of GDP, or about $600 billion in that year. An additional consideration is that lawmakers might determine that current economic conditions call for new policies that would increase deficits in the next few years. If such policies were enacted, then reducing debt held by the public to a particular level in 2021 would require even greater deficit reduction in later years.

The Timing of Deficit Reduction

Policymakers face difficult trade-offs in decisions about how quickly to implement policies to reduce budget deficits, as the impacts on people and the economy depend crucially on the timing of the changes. In confronting those trade-offs, policymakers could consider the relative disadvantages of reducing deficits slowly or quickly, the economic effects of deficit reduction achieved on alternative time paths, and ways to reconcile near-term and longer-term economic objectives. Although there are trade-offs in choosing the timing of policy changes to reduce future deficits, such trade-offs do not apply to the timing of decisions about the changes. Rather, there are important benefits and few apparent costs to deciding now what policy actions will be taken to resolve the longer-term budgetary imbalance. Enacting policy changes soon would allow for implementing them gradually while still limiting further increases in federal debt and the corresponding negative consequences. Moreover, the enactment of credible policy changes that reduce deficits in the future would probably increase economic activity in the near term by boosting confidence and holding down interest rates.

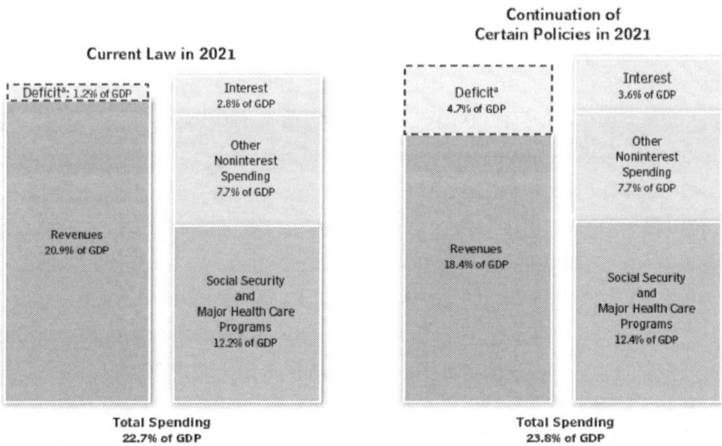

Source: Congressional Budget Office.

Notes: The projection with the continuation of certain policies is based on several assumptions: first, that most of the provisions of the Tax Relief, Unemployment Insurance Reauthorization, and Job Creation Act of 2010 that originally were enacted in 2001, 2003, 2009, and 2010 do not expire on December 31, 2012, but instead continue; second, that the alternative minimum tax is indexed for inflation after 2011; and third, that Medicare's payment rates for physicians are held constant at their 2011 level. Continuing the tax provisions would also increase outlays for refundable tax credits; however, the effect on outlays is shown in the revenue portion of the bar.

Major health care programs include Medicare, Medicaid, the Children's Health Insurance Program, and exchange subsidies and related spending.

GDP = gross domestic product.

a. In this figure, the deficit does not equal total spending minus revenues in 2021 because it has been reduced by incorporating effects of provisions related to the Joint Select Committee on Deficit Reduction. The Budget Control Act of 2011 (Public Law 112-25) created that committee to propose further deficit reduction totaling at least $1.5 trillion over 10 years. The act also specified automatic procedures for reducing spending by as much as $1.2 trillion if legislation originating with the new deficit reduction committee does not achieve savings of at least $1.2 trillion. CBO has incorporated that amount of deficit reduction in its baseline (including an amount equal to 0.7 percent of GDP in 2021, which includes savings in debt-service costs) but has no basis for allocating that amount between revenues and outlays. Accordingly, outlay and revenue projections included here exclude the effects of those provisions; the deficit projection, however, includes the effects.

Figure 7. Federal Revenues and Spending in 2021 Under CBO's Baseline or with a Continuation of Certain Policies.

Disadvantages of Reducing Deficits Slowly

On the one hand, reducing deficits slowly would have some negative consequences. First, implementing spending cuts or tax increases gradually, rather than abruptly, would lead to a greater accumulation of government debt, which would have a number of costs:

- Rising debt would cause a growing portion of people's savings to go to purchase government debt rather than to finance investments in productive capital such as factories and computers. Specifically, larger federal deficits imply, all else being equal, lower national saving; that lower saving reduces the capital stock owned by U.S. citizens over time through a decrease in domestic investment, an increase in net borrowing from abroad, or both. That crowding out of investment in productive capital would lead to lower output and incomes than would otherwise occur.[21]
- Higher levels of debt imply higher interest payments on that debt, which would eventually require either higher taxes or a reduction in government benefits and services.
- Rising debt would increasingly restrict policymakers' ability to use tax and spending policies to respond to unexpected challenges, such as economic downturns, financial turmoil, or international crises. As a result, the effects of such developments on the economy and people's well-being could be worse.
- Growing debt also would increase the probability of a sudden fiscal crisis, during which investors would lose confidence in the government's ability to manage its budget and the government would thereby lose its ability to borrow at affordable rates. Such a crisis would confront policymakers with extremely difficult choices. To restore investors' confidence, policymakers would probably need to enact spending cuts or tax increases more drastic and painful than those that would have been necessary had the adjustments come sooner.

Second, gradual spending cuts or tax increases might reduce the credibility of the intended deficit reduction. Households, businesses, state and local governments, and financial market participants might be skeptical that unpleasant policy changes that were announced but deferred well into the future would ever take effect. Instead, those observers might expect that those changes would be altered before they occurred. Such expectations might be reinforced by recent experience, in which the expiration of provisions that restrain individual income tax revenues were extended, the expanding reach of the AMT under existing law was checked, and looming cuts in Medicare's payments to physicians under existing law were avoided. In each of those policy areas, lawmakers have acted to extend existing policies rather than to follow current law.

Lessening the credibility of future deficit reduction would diminish the favorable effects of such policy changes in the near term. If there is widespread belief that cuts in spending or increases in taxes were going to happen in the future, that expectation would help to hold down current medium-term and long-term interest rates. Those lower interest rates would tend to increase spending and investing by households and businesses, other things being equal. However, if people did not believe that promised changes in policy would actually take effect, those advantages would be diminished or lost. In order to increase the credibility of future deficit reduction, policymakers could enact specific policy changes into law and show that those changes had fairly widespread support.

Disadvantages of Reducing Deficits Quickly

On the other hand, reducing deficits quickly would have some negative consequences as well. First, implementing spending cuts or tax increases abruptly would give families, businesses, and state and local governments little time to plan and adjust. Deficit reduction inevitably involves some combination of scaling back government benefits, shrinking government contracts or payrolls, reducing grants to state and local governments, or raising tax collections. The households, businesses, and other levels of government that would be affected by such changes would need to adjust their own spending habits, work behavior, investment and hiring decisions, or tax policies—perhaps in significant ways. Therefore, they would benefit from advance notice so they would have some flexibility in how and when they can alter their behavior.

Older generations would have particular difficulty adapting to immediate spending cuts or tax increases because their opportunity to adjust their work or saving is more limited.[22] As a result, a common feature of proposals to change programs that affect older Americans—including Social Security, Medicare, and Medicaid—is to limit the impact of such changes on people who are currently over certain ages. (Of course, limiting the impact of policy changes on the current elderly would reduce the amount of savings that could be achieved in the near term and might, for a given amount of cumulative deficit reduction, increase the extent of the policy changes that would be imposed later on current young people.) Moreover, the ability of many households, firms, and state and local governments to adjust to cutbacks in federal spending or increases in federal taxes may be more limited now than at other times because of the strained financial circumstances in which many find themselves.

Second, and particularly important given the current state of the economy, immediate spending cuts or tax increases would represent an added drag on the weak economic expansion. When the economy has substantial unemployment, as well as unused factories, offices, and equipment, reductions in aggregate demand (the total purchases of a country's output of goods and services by consumers, businesses, governments, and foreigners) generally widen the gap between the economy's actual level of output and its potential (a level that corresponds to a high rate of use of labor and capital). Decreasing federal spending or increasing federal taxes now would tend to reduce aggregate demand and thereby lead to less output and employment in the next few years.

For example, cutting federal purchases of goods and services subtracts from the demand for goods and services directly, and reducing federal transfers to people (such as unemployment insurance payments or Social Security benefits) or to states and localities (such as support for secondary education) tends to decrease the amount of goods and services purchased by the recipients. Similarly, raising tax collections tends to decrease the spending of the people paying those taxes.

The extent to which deficit reduction lessens demand depends on the details of the policies enacted and on the economic situation.[23] For example, when the Federal Reserve's ability to lower short-term interest rates is constrained because those rates are already near zero, as they are currently, the short-run effects of changes in government spending and taxes on output tend to be larger than usual. Nevertheless, changes in government spending and taxes usually affect demand only temporarily: They raise or lower output relative to potential only for a while because, over time, stabilizing forces in the economy (such as the responses of prices and interest rates and actions by the Federal Reserve) tend to move output back toward its potential.

Quantifying the Economic Effects of Deficit Reduction

Although cuts in government spending or increases in taxes in the next few years would, by themselves, reduce output and employment during that period, credible steps to narrow budget deficits over the longer term would tend to boost output and employment in the next few years by holding down interest rates and by reducing uncertainty and enhancing business and consumer confidence. Therefore, the near-term economic effects of deficit reduction would depend on the balance between changes in spending and taxes that take effect quickly and those that take effect gradually. According to CBO's analysis, credible policy changes that would substantially reduce deficits later in the coming decade and over the long term—without immediate cuts in spending or increases in taxes— would both support the economic expansion in the next few years and strengthen the economy over the longer term.

A recent analysis by CBO provides a rough indication of the magnitude of the economic effects of reducing deficits along a hypothetical time path under current economic conditions.[24] In that analysis, the agency estimated the short-term and longer-term effects of reducing the primary deficit (the budget deficit excluding net interest) by $100 billion in 2012 and by amounts increasing gradually to $300 billion by 2021 (without any particular changes in spending or revenues specified). According to the agency's estimates, that illustrative plan would decrease real gross national product (GNP) in 2012, 2013, and 2014 by amounts ranging from roughly 0.1 percent to 0.6 percent depending on the year and the assumptions used.[25] However, the increases in national saving and investment that would result from smaller deficits were estimated to increase real GNP by roughly 0.4 percent to 1.4 percent from 2019 through 2021.[26]

A different policy that had the same amount of cumulative reduction in primary deficits but that reduced deficits more slowly than the policy analyzed would have more favorable macroeconomic effects in the next few years. However, that alternative policy would have less favorable effects later in the decade because the total budgetary impact of slower deficit reduction would be smaller?a result of the policy's smaller impact on interest and the slower reduction in debt relative to what would otherwise occur, causing the savings in interest costs to compound more slowly. Those differences in macroeconomic effects later in the decade could be offset by undertaking slightly more cumulative reduction in primary deficits.

The economic effects of policies that reduce budget deficits sharply given current economic conditions can be seen by comparing CBO's baseline economic projections under current law with economic projections under a different set of policies. Under current law, most of the provisions in the 2010 tax act expire at the end of 2011 or 2012, the reach of the AMT expands greatly at the end of 2011, and Medicare's payment rates for physicians' services fall sharply at the end of 2011; those policies help to reduce deficits sharply, but CBO also expects them to reduce economic growth in the near term. Suppose, instead, that most of the cuts in individual income taxes and estate and gift taxes now scheduled to expire in 2012 or 2013 are extended through 2021, limits to the reach of the AMT that are set to expire at the end of 2011 are also continued through 2021, and Medicare's payment rates for physicians are maintained at their 2011 levels. Under those alternative assumptions, CBO estimates that real GDP in 2013 would be between 0.6 percent and 2.3 percent more than projected under current law.[27] Higher real GDP would result in a lower unemployment rate and somewhat higher interest rates over the next few years than would occur with the smaller deficits projected in the baseline.

However, unless other policy changes were enacted, real GDP would be higher in CBO's baseline projections by later in the decade than under that set of alternative policies. The lower marginal tax rates under those policies would increase people's incentives to work and save, but the significantly larger budget deficits would crowd out private investment in productive capital. By the end of 2021, as the effect of larger budget deficits outweighed that of lower tax rates, real GDP would be between 0.3 percent and 1.9 percent smaller than it would be under current law, CBO estimates. Without other policy changes, the budget would be on an unsustainable path under those policies, and the negative effects on output and incomes would rise further after 2021.

Reconciling Near-Term and Longer-Term Objectives

Some policymakers and analysts have advocated near-term reductions in taxes or increases in federal spending to increase output and employment in the next few years. Such policies might or might not worsen the medium-term and long-term fiscal outlook depending on whether other changes in policy were enacted at the same time and on what those other changes were. However, there is no inherent contradiction between using fiscal policy to support the economy today, while the unemployment rate is high and many factories and offices are underused, and imposing fiscal restraint several years from now, when output and employment will probably be close to their potential.[28] What would such an approach mean in practice?

If taxes were cut permanently or government spending was increased permanently, and no other changes were made to fiscal policy, the economy would suffer in the medium term and long term. Indeed, if people believed that policy changes that increased near-term deficits presaged larger budget deficits in the medium term and long term, and thus that the federal budget outlook had become even bleaker, the economy could be hurt in the near term by a faltering of business and consumer confidence and an increase in interest rates. Moreover, even if tax cuts or spending increases were temporary, the additional debt accumulated during that temporary period would weigh on the budget and the economy over time.

Therefore, if policymakers wanted to achieve both a short-term economic boost and medium-term and long-term fiscal sustainability, a combination of policies would be required: changes in taxes and spending that would widen the deficit now but reduce it later in the decade. Such an approach would work best if the future policy changes were sufficiently specific and widely supported so that households, businesses, state and local governments, and participants in financial markets believed that the future fiscal restraint would truly take effect.

The Composition of Deficit Reduction

As policymakers consider the composition of policy changes to be used to reduce budget deficits, many factors may play a role. The most fundamental question is what role the government should play in the U.S. economy and society. The amount and composition of federal spending and revenues affect the total amount and types of output that are produced and consumed in the country, the distribution of those material resources among various segments of society, and people's well-being in a variety of ways.[29] In particular, policymakers may be influenced by the historical patterns of spending and revenues and by the economic impacts of alternative spending and tax policies.

Projected Spending and Revenues in Historical Context

In considering the challenge of putting fiscal policy on a sustainable path, many observers have wondered whether it is possible to return to policies regarding federal spending and revenues that, in earlier years, usually generated deficits that were small relative to GDP and kept the amount of debt held by the public to between about one-quarter and one-half of GDP.

Looking for historical reference points is natural. However, the past combination of policies cannot be repeated when it comes to the federal budget: The aging of the population and rising costs for health care have changed the backdrop for federal budget policy in a fundamental way. To see this point most clearly, it is useful to consider the historical experience and CBO's projections for three broad categories of the budget: revenues; spending for Social Security, Medicare, and other major health care programs; and all other spending excluding interest payments.

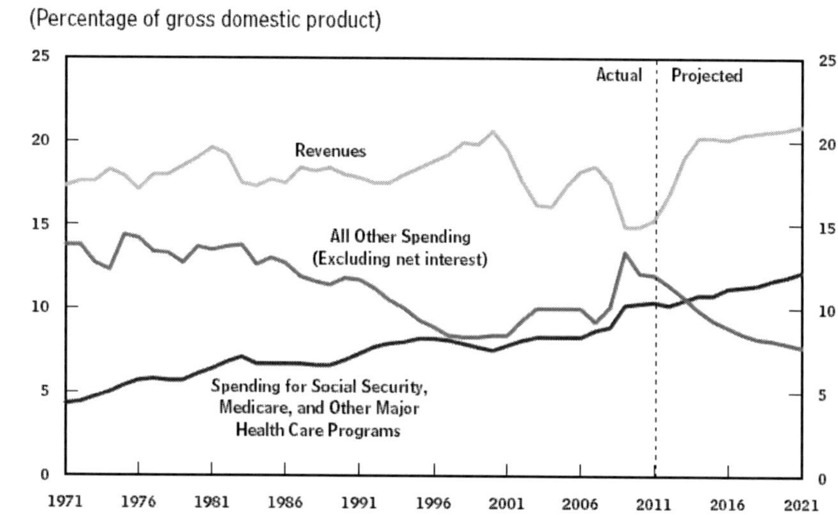

Source: Congressional Budget Office.

Note: Other major health care programs include Medicaid, the Children's Health Insurance Program, and exchanges subsidies and related spending.

Figure 8. Revenues and Spending, Excluding Interest.

Federal Revenues

Revenues have averaged 18.0 percent of GDP during the past 40 years (see Figure 8). They have varied substantially around that level but show no clear trend. Under current law, revenues equal 15.3 percent of GDP in 2011 and will rise to about 21 percent of GDP in 2021; if, instead, all of the tax provisions that are scheduled to expire under current law were extended, revenues in 2021 would be close to their historical average of 18 percent.

Individual income tax receipts account for most of the projected increase in federal revenues over the coming decade, largely because of scheduled changes in tax law and features of the tax system that cause revenues to rise faster than income over time, as well as projected increases in receipts that reflect an expected rebound in taxable income and some other effects of the economic recovery (see Figure 9). As a result, individual income tax receipts increase steadily in CBO's baseline, from 7.2 percent of GDP in 2011 to 11.2 percent in 2021. By comparison, such receipts stood at 8.0 percent in 1971. Receipts from both social insurance and corporate income taxes are projected to increase modestly relative to GDP over the next 10 years, remaining in the vicinity of their 40-year averages, CBO projects.

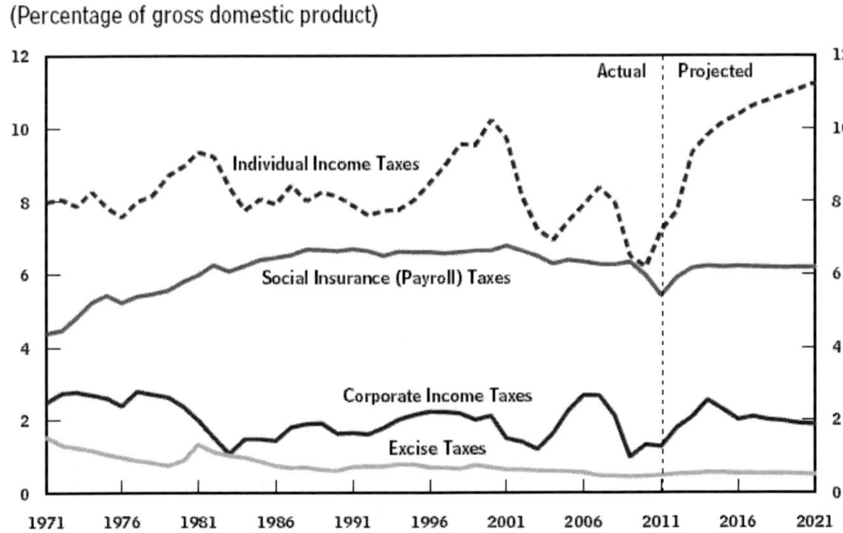

Source: Congressional Budget Office.

Figure 9. Revenues by Source.

Two additional perspectives on the evolution of the federal tax system during the past several decades are provided by changes in the burden of taxes on households at different points in the distribution of income and by changes in tax rates that affect the after-tax return to additional work or saving.[30] Households generally bear the economic cost, or burden, of the taxes that they pay directly, such as individual income taxes (including taxes paid on dividends, interest, and capital gains) and employees' share of payroll taxes. Households also bear the burden of the taxes paid by businesses; in particular, in CBO's judgment (and that of most economists), employers' share of payroll taxes is passed on to employees in the form of lower wages. One measure of the tax burden is the average tax rate—that is, the taxes paid as a share of income.

Federal taxes are progressive: Average federal tax rates generally rise with income. In 2007 (the most recent year for which data are available), households in the bottom fifth, or quintile, of the income distribution (with average income of $18,400, under a broad definition of income) paid about 4 percent of their income in federal taxes, while the middle quintile, with average income of $64,500, paid 14 percent, and the highest quintile, with average income of $264,700, paid 25 percent (see Figure 10). Between 1979 and 2007, average tax rates declined, on balance, for households in each quintile of the income distribution.

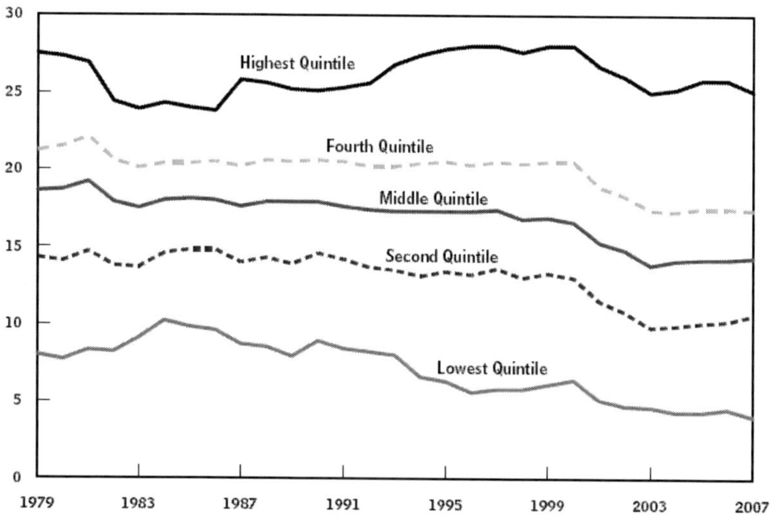

Source: Congressional Budget Office.

Note: For information on the calculation of average tax rates, the ranking of households, and the allocation of taxes, see Congressional Budget Office, *Average Federal Tax Rates in 2007* (June 2010).

Figure 10. Average Federal Tax Rates, by Income Quintile, 1979 to 2007.

One measure of the effect of taxes on the returns from working and saving is the marginal tax rate—the tax paid per dollar of extra earnings or dollar of extra income from savings. For a representative family of four with median income, the marginal tax rate on earnings (combining the rates for both federal income and payroll taxes) 40 years ago was around 20 percent (see Figure 11). That rate climbed over the next 10 years as a result of rising payroll tax rates and inflation-driven increases in nominal incomes, which pushed median-income families into higher tax brackets. Following a reduction in income tax rates in 1986, the marginal tax rate for a representative median-income family has remained at about 30 percent (the rate is 2 percentage points lower in 2011 with the temporary reduction in the payroll tax rate). The marginal tax rate on income from savings has also fallen, on balance, over the past 40 years owing to reductions in statutory tax rates on overall taxable income as well as separate reductions in the tax rates that apply to income from capital gains and dividends.

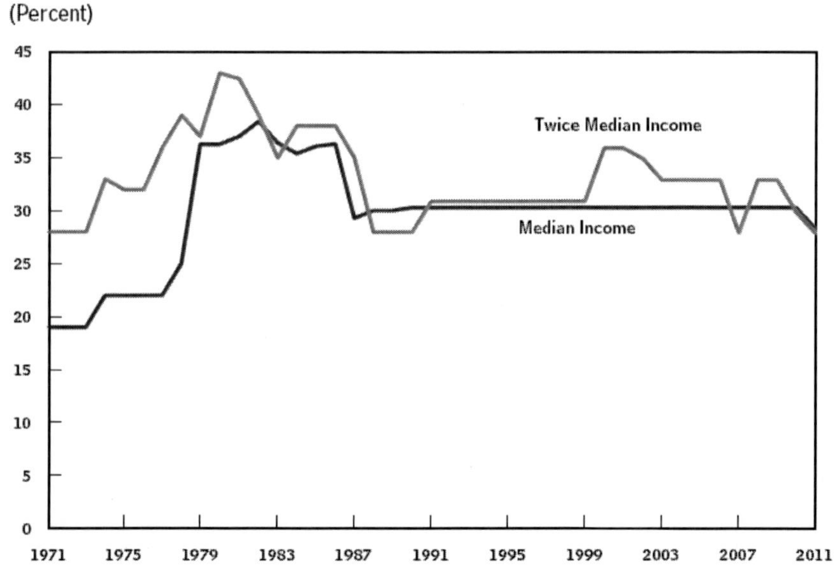

Sources: Department of the Treasury, Office of Tax Analysis; Congressional Budget Office.

Figure 11. Marginal Tax Rates (Income and Payroll) on Earnings for a Family of Four with a Single Earner, 1971 to 2011.

Social Security and Major Health Care Programs

Spending on Social Security and the major health care programs—Medicare, Medicaid, the Children's Health Insurance Program, and insurance subsidies to be provided through exchanges in coming years—will be 12.2 percent of GDP in 2021, according to CBO's projections based on current law. Such spending equals 10.4 percent of GDP in 2011 and represented an average of 7.2 percent of GDP during the past 40 years. The marked increases in such spending experienced during the past 40 years and projected for the next 10 years reflect the aging of the population, rising costs for health care, and changes in federal programs. Spending for Social Security, which totaled 3.3 percent of GDP in 1971, will equal 4.8 percent in 2011 and is projected to continue growing over the next 10 years, reaching 5.4 percent in 2021 (see Figure 12). Medicare spending (excluding offsetting receipts) is projected to grow even faster, relative to the overall economy, from 0.7 percent of GDP in 1971 to 3.7 percent in 2011 and 4.1 percent in 2021. CBO projects that spending for other major health care programs will rise from 1.7 percent of GDP in 2012 to 2.8 percent in 2021; by comparison, Medicaid spending represented 0.3 percent of GDP in 1971.

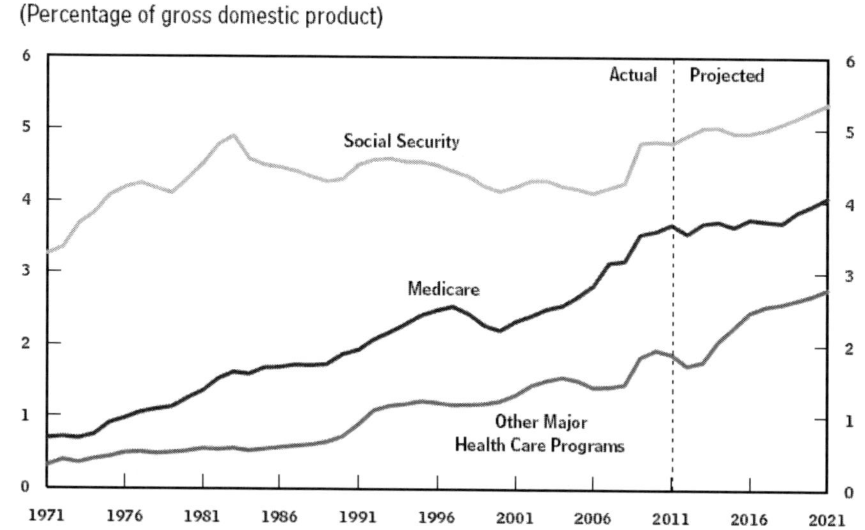

Source: Congressional Budget Office.

Note: Other major health care programs include Medicaid, the Children's Health Insurance Program, and exchange subsidies and related spending.

Figure 12. Spending for Social Security, Medicare, and Other Major Health Care Programs.

Most of the spending for Social Security and the major health care programs goes to benefits for people over age 65, with smaller shares for blind and disabled people and for nonelderly able-bodied people. Specifically, CBO estimates that more than four-fifths of Social Security spending in 2021 will go to benefits for retired workers and their dependents and survivors, with the remaining less than one-fifth going to benefits for disabled workers and their spouses and children. In addition, even with the significant expansion of federal support for health care for lower-income people enacted in last year's legislation, CBO projects that about half of spending for the major health care programs in 2021 will go to people over age 65, with another quarter going to the blind and disabled, and the remaining quarter going to able-bodied nonelderly people.

Other Federal Spending

All spending apart from that for Social Security, the major health care programs, and interest payments on the debt has averaged 11.5 percent of GDP during the past 40 years and equals 12.0 percent in 2011. That broad category includes some mandatory spending as well as all of defense and nondefense discretionary spending. That mandatory spending includes various income security programs, retirement benefits, and other outlays. Defense spending is by far the largest single piece of the broad category, and nondefense discretionary spending includes transportation, health research, education and training, and other programs. Given the assumptions that govern CBO's baseline projections, spending for all of these programs together is projected to equal 7.7 percent of GDP in 2021, the lowest as a share of GDP in the past 40 years.

The mandatory spending in that category is spending apart from that on Social Security and the major health care programs—specifically, outlays for the Supplemental Nutrition Assistance Program (formerly known as Food Stamps), unemployment compensation, some veterans' benefits, federal civilian and military retirement benefits, and other programs (including offsetting receipts). Such spending averaged 2.7 percent of GDP during the past 40 years and totals 3.0 percent in 2011 (see Figure 13). Expected improvement in the economy and other factors reduces that spending to 1.6 percent of GDP by 2021 in CBO's baseline projections.

Discretionary spending, which stood at 11.3 percent of GDP in 1971, will total 9.0 percent in 2011. As a result of the caps put in place by the Budget Control Act (and apart from any further reduction in caps triggered by the enforcement provisions of the act), such spending will fall sharply relative to the size of the economy over the next 10 years, reaching 6.1 percent in 2021, CBO projects. That reduction in discretionary spending could be achieved by many different combinations of defense and nondefense appropriations. For example, if defense and nondefense appropriations (excluding war-related funding) were reduced proportionately, relative to the funding that would be necessary to keep pace with inflation, defense spending would total 3.4 percent of GDP in 2021 while nondefense spending would equal 2.7 percent, CBO estimates. By comparison, in 1971, defense and nondefense spending totaled 7.3 percent and 4.0 percent of GDP. Many other combinations of defense and nondefense funding are possible under the caps.

Implications for Future Budget Policy

Combining the various components of spending, total federal spending excluding net interest will represent 19.9 percent of GDP in 2021, according to CBO's projections under current law, a bit above the 40-year average of 18.6 percent (see Figure 14). And the composition of that spending will be noticeably different from what the nation has experienced in recent decades: Spending for Social Security and the major health care programs will be much higher, and spending for all other federal programs and activities, except for net interest payments, will be much lower. Alternatively, if the laws governing Social Security and the major health care programs were unchanged, and all other programs were operated in line with their average relationship to the size of the economy during the past 40 years, total federal spending would be projected to be much higher in 2021— nearly 24 percent of GDP. That amount exceeds the 40-year average for revenues as a share of GDP by nearly 6 percentage points—even before interest payments on the debt have been included.

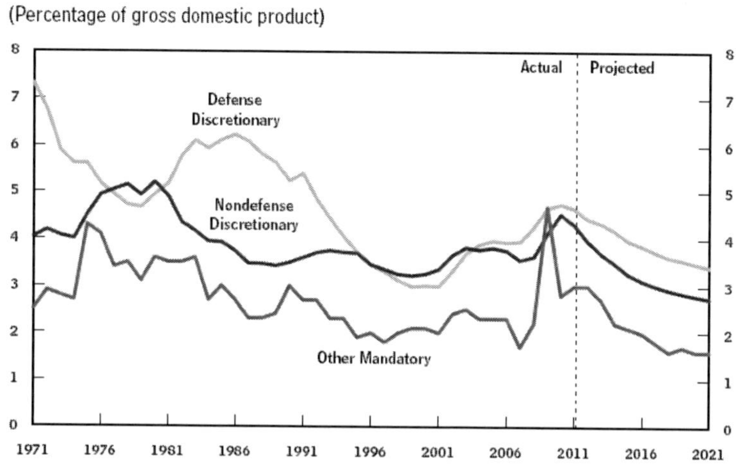

Source: Congressional Budget Office.

Notes: Other federal spending includes discretionary spending (both defense and nondefense) and mandatory spending besides that for Social Security and Medicare and other major health care programs (as shown in Figure 12) as well as interest payments on debt held by the public.

When constructing its baseline, CBO assumes that discretionary appropriations will adhere to the statutory caps recently enacted into law by the Budget Control Act of 2011 (Public Law 112-25). Because the caps do not constrain appropriations for military operations in Afghanistan and Iraq (or for similar activities), such outlays are assumed to equal $159 billion (the amount provided for 2011), adjusted in future years for inflation. In this figure, all other funding is assumed to be reduced proportionately, relative to the funding that would be necessary to keep pace with inflation, in order to keep total discretionary funding within the caps on appropriations other than those for war-related purposes.

Figure 13. Other Federal Spending, by Category.

At the same time, the sharp increase in federal debt and a return to more-normal interest rates will boost the government's net interest costs. They are projected to reach 2.8 percent of GDP in 2021, compared with only 1.5 percent of GDP in 2011 and an average of 2.2 percent of GDP during the past 40 years.

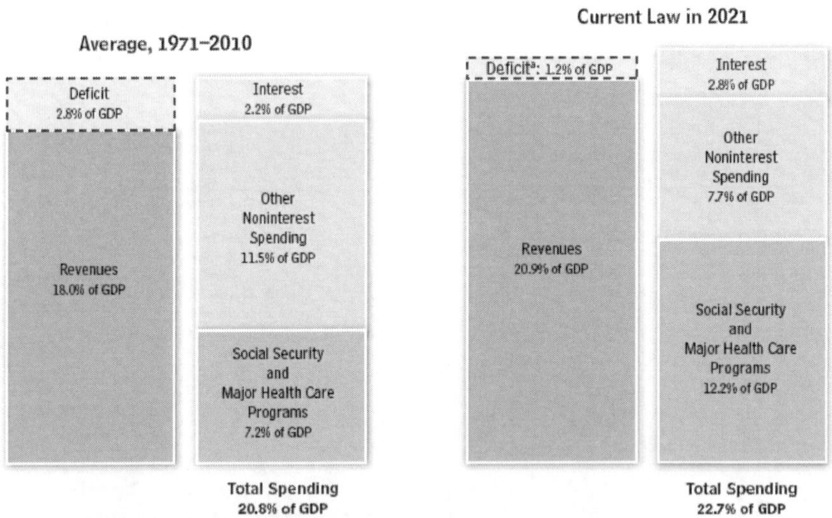

Source: Congressional Budget Office.

Notes: Major health care programs include Medicare, Medicaid, the Children's Health Insurance Program, and exchange subsidies and related spending.

GDP = gross domestic product.

a. In this figure, the deficit does not equal total spending minus revenue in 2021 because it has been reduced by incorporating effects of provisions related to the Joint Select Committee on Deficit Reduction. The Budget Control Act of 2011 (Public Law 112-25) created that committee to propose further deficit reduction totaling at least $1.5 trillion over 10 years. The act also specified automatic procedures for reducing spending by as much as $1.2 trillion if legislation originating with the new deficit reduction committee does not achieve savings of at least $1.2 trillion. CBO has incorporated that amount of deficit reduction in its baseline (including an amount equal to 0.7 percent of GDP in 2021, which includes savings in debt-service costs) but has no basis for allocating that amount between revenues and outlays. Accordingly, outlay and revenue projections included here exclude the effects of those provisions; the deficit projection, however, includes the effects.

Figure 14. Federal Revenues and Spending Historically and in 2021 Under CBO's Baseline.

What do those numbers imply about the choices that policymakers—and citizens— confront about future policies? Given the aging of the population and the rising costs for health care, attaining a sustainable budget for the federal government will require the United States to deviate from the policies of the past 40 years in at least one of the following ways:

- Raise federal revenues significantly above their average share of GDP;
- Make major changes to the sorts of benefits provided for Americans when they become older; or
- Substantially reduce the role of the rest of the federal government—that is, defense, the Supplemental Nutrition Assistance Program, unemployment compensation, support for blind and disabled people, other income-security programs, health care programs for people under age 65, veterans' benefits, federal civilian and military retirement benefits, transportation, health research, education and training, and other programs—relative to the size of the economy.

Economic Effects of the Composition of Deficit Reduction

The effects of deficit reduction on the economy would depend not just on the timing of changes in federal spending and taxes, as discussed earlier, but also on the composition of those changes.

In the near term, with a large amount of unused resources in the U.S. economy and short-term interest rates near zero, the principal channel through which policy changes will affect output and employment is through their impact on the economy's overall demand for goods and services. Changes in different types of federal spending and different types of federal taxes could have very different impacts on demand, as CBO has estimated previously.[31] Policies that would generally reduce near-term output and employment the most per dollar of budgetary savings are those that are implemented relatively quickly; have the largest effect on people whose consumption tends to be restricted by their income; or withdraw a time-limited incentive for households, businesses, or state and local governments to increase their spending.

In the medium term and long term, the principal channel through which policy changes would affect output and employment is through their impact on the economy's potential output. Over the long run, the nation's potential to produce goods and services depends on the size and quality of its labor force, on the stock of productive capital (such as factories, vehicles, and computers), and on the efficiency with which labor and capital are used to produce goods and services. The nation's capital stock depends both on public saving (the surpluses, if any, of state and local governments and the federal government) and on private saving (by households and businesses). Efficiency depends on such factors such as production technology, the way businesses are organized, and the regulatory environment. Thus, the federal government's tax and spending policies affect potential output by altering the size and quality of the labor force, the amount of public and private saving, and the efficiency with which labor and capital are combined.

Smaller federal deficits owing to any combination of spending and tax policies imply greater public saving and, other effects aside, national saving. An overall increase in national saving expands the capital stock owned by U.S. citizens over time through an increase in domestic investment, a decrease in net borrowing from abroad, or both. However, changes in spending or tax policies can have other significant effects on potential output depending on the specific nature of those changes.

The Economic Impact of Increases in Federal Tax Revenues

Changes in tax policy can affect the incentives for individuals and businesses to save and invest. Increasing effective marginal tax rates on capital income (income derived from wealth, such as stock dividends, realized capital gains, or the owner's profits from a business) would reduce the after-tax rate of return on saving and therefore affect the amount of saving that people chose to do.[32] Specifically, a reduction in the after-tax return on saving would influence private saving in two opposing ways: Lower after-tax returns would tend to decrease saving, but they also would reduce the value of existing assets, making households poorer and thus tending to encourage saving. On balance, the combined effect on saving of lower after-tax returns can be positive or negative, and researchers generally conclude that the effect is small. CBO, in its analyses, projects that increases in marginal tax rates on capital income reduce saving by a small amount.[33]

Changes in corporate tax rules can affect the effective marginal tax rates on investments in different forms of physical capital (equipment, software, and structures) and in research and development related to new types of goods and services and methods of production. They can also affect the organization of production: Because the corporate income tax does not apply to all businesses (for example, it exempts partnerships, sole proprietorships, and corporations with a limited number of shareholders), changes in corporate tax rules can affect how businesses are organized, which can affect the efficiency of the allocation of resources. In addition, corporate tax rules can affect multinational corporations' decisions about where to invest. A country with a relatively high corporate tax rate stands to lose investment to lower-tax countries, and less investment may reduce the amount of capital available to workers and thus reduce wages. Even if the location of investment does not change, the tax base of a country with a relatively high corporate tax rate may erode because businesses can reduce their taxes by recharacterizing where their income is earned to place relatively more of it in low-tax countries.

Changes in tax policy can also affect the incentives for individuals to work or for individuals and firms to invest in the education and skills of the workforce. Increasing effective marginal tax rates on labor income would reduce the after-tax return on work and therefore affect the amount of work that people chose to do. As with a reduction in the after-tax return on saving, a reduction in after-tax earnings would influence labor supply in two opposing ways: Lower after-tax earnings would tend to decrease working because workers would receive less for each extra hour of labor they supplied, but lower after-tax earnings also would reduce workers' earnings for any given amount of work, making it difficult to sustain a certain standard of living and thus tending to encourage additional work. For many people, the opposing incentives from increasing marginal tax rates largely offset each other, although most economists conclude that, on average, the negative effects of lower after-tax earnings for each additional hour worked slightly outweigh the positive effects of lower after-tax earnings from current working hours. Responses to changes in tax rates can also vary among family members, with secondary earners (for example, the spouse of a household's primary bread-winner) generally responding to a greater extent than primary earners. CBO, in its analyses, projects that increases in marginal tax rates on labor income decrease modestly the hours of labor that workers supply.

Rather than, or in addition to, changes to tax rates, changes in tax policy could involve revisions to other aspects of the tax code. A variety of exclusions, deductions, and exemptions in both the federal individual and corporate income taxes cause the individual and corporate income tax bases—the amount of income subject to taxation—to be significantly smaller than the income reported on tax returns. The most comprehensive measure of income reported on individual income tax returns is gross income—and even that measure omits certain types of personal income that taxpayers are allowed to exclude from reporting. Gross income totaled $8.4 trillion in 2008, but once the allowable deductions and exemptions were subtracted, total income subject to tax (taxable income) was $5.7 trillion—or 67 percent of gross income. In addition to the exclusions, deductions, and exemptions, both the individual and the corporate income tax allow for tax credits that reduce the final tax directly paid by households and businesses. All else being equal, those provisions of tax law reduce tax receipts by hundreds of billions of dollars each year; as a result, tax rates must be higher to collect the same amount of revenues that would be collected in the absence of those provisions.

Income tax exclusions, deductions, exemptions, and credits generally fall into three broad categories: those that modify taxable income to exclude the costs of earning that income, such as an employee's deduction for work-related expenses; those that subsidize or promote certain uses of income that are deemed worthy, such as the deduction for charitable contributions; and those that provide tax relief on the basis of certain income or demographic characteristics, such as the earned income tax credit for lower-income working families and the child tax credit for families with children. Some of those tax provisions are termed "tax expenditures" because they are similar in some ways to government spending. Like spending programs, tax expenditures provide financial assistance to particular activities, entities, or groups of people. They are more similar to entitlement programs than to discretionary spending because they are not subject to annual appropriations and any person or entity that meets the requirements can receive the benefits.

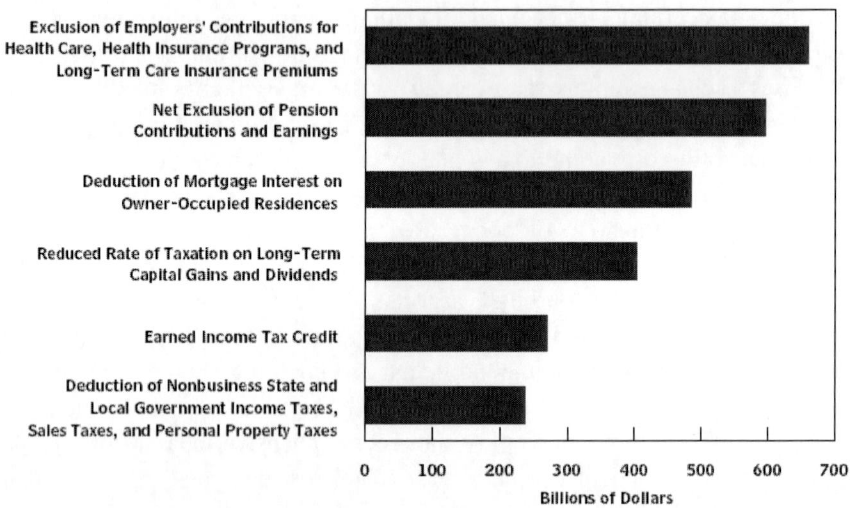

Source: Joint Committee on Taxation.

Figure 15. Cumulative Budgetary Effect of Major Income Tax Expenditures, 2010 to 2014.

Raising tax revenues by reducing tax expenditures would, for many existing expenditures, enhance the allocation of resources and therefore be good for the economy. According to estimates by the staff of the Joint Committee on Taxation, the three largest tax expenditures in the individual income tax law are those providing preferential treatment for employment-based health insurance, retirement savings, and home ownership (see Figure 15). Each of those tax expenditures may help achieve certain societal goals: a healthier population, adequate financial resources for retirement, and stable communities of homeowners. But uncapped tax expenditures may also encourage overconsumption of the favored good or subsidize activity that would have taken place without the tax incentives. For example, those three income tax expenditures may prompt people to consume more health services than are necessary, reallocate existing savings from accounts that are not tax-preferred to retirement accounts, and acquire mortgages and purchase homes beyond their needs.

The Economic Impact of Reductions in Federal Spending

Changes in government spending can affect potential output as well. Some types of spending, such as funding for improvements to roads and highways, may add to the economy's potential output in much the same way that private capital investment does. Other government programs, such as funding for grants to increase access to college education, may raise long-term productivity by enhancing people's skills. Reducing spending in those areas might reduce potential output. Even among types of federal spending that contribute to potential output, the effects of different policies can vary greatly. For example, spending for basic research and education may affect output only after a number of years, but once those investments begin to boost output, they may pay off over more years than would the average investment in physical capital (in economic terms, they may have a low rate of depreciation). Moreover, even within a specific program, how those funds are allocated also matters a great deal. Although some specific government investments in a particular category may be as productive as private investment, other projects probably fall short of that benchmark.

On a more fundamental level, the government provides a crucial role in maintaining the legal and institutional framework within which the economy operates. Government spending on the justice system, for example, supports the smooth functioning of the economy by protecting private property rights and enforcing contracts. Cutbacks in such spending could diminish potential output.

End Notes

[1] The *Blue Chip* consensus is the average of about 50 forecasts by private-sector economists.

[2] See Congressional Budget Office, *The Budget and Economic Outlook: An Update* (August 2011).

[3] Although real GDP grew at an average annual rate of 0.7 percent in the first half of this year, CBO anticipates it will grow at about 2.0 percent in the second half.

[4] For a review of evidence suggesting that real gross domestic income is a more accurate indicator of current economic activity than real GDP, see Jeremy J. Nalewaik, "The Income- and Expenditure-Side Estimates of U.S. Output Growth," *Brookings Papers on Economic Activity* (Spring 2010), pp. 71–106.

[5] CBO has not prepared new estimates of the paths for potential GDP and the output gap since it published its previous estimates in August.

[6] The natural rate of unemployment is the rate arising from all sources except cyclical fluctuations in the economywide demand for goods and services.

[7] For an analysis of the cost of losing a job in an economic downturn, see Congressional Budget Office, *Losing a Job During a Recession*, Issue Brief (April 2010). For a discussion of other measures of weakness in the labor market, including the number of people who have recently been employed part time but want full-time work, see Congressional Budget Office, *The Budget and Economic Outlook: An Update* (August 2011), pp. 47–48.

[8] Budget estimates are provided for fiscal years, which span the period of October 1 through September 30, while the economic outlook discussion presents information on a calendar year basis.

[9] The budget projections discussed here are those that CBO reported in August 2011 and are based on the economic forecast that the agency issued at that time. For a more detailed discussion of those projections, see Congressional Budget Office, *The Budget and Economic Outlook: An Update* (August 2011).

[10] Outlays refer to spending to pay a federal obligation.

[11] That alternative is based on an assumption that the lower tax rates, expanded credits, and higher deductions enacted in 2001, 2003, and 2009 and then extended through 2012 by the 2010 tax act are made permanent. It also reflects an assumption that the estate and gift tax rules for 2011 and 2012 (as established by the 2010 tax act) continue permanently beyond their currently scheduled expiration in 2012. Furthermore, it incorporates an assumption that the higher AMT exemption contained in the 2010 tax act does not expire at the end of 2011 and is indexed to inflation thereafter. Finally, it does not incorporate any changes in revenues that may result from the work of the deficit reduction committee.

[12] Those earlier projections are shown in Congressional Budget Office, *An Analysis of the President's Budgetary Proposals for Fiscal Year 2012* (April 2011). For an analysis of the Budget Control Act of 2011, see Congressional Budget Office, letter to the Honorable John A. Boehner and the Honorable Harry Reid estimating the impact on the deficit of the Budget Control Act of 2011 (August 1, 2011). The estimates discussed here do not include the effect of initiatives in the Budget Control Act to enhance "program integrity," which depend on future appropriations and will be incorporated into CBO's baseline if they are implemented in the future.

[13] Budget authority (or "funding") refers to the authority provided by law to incur financial obligations, which eventually result in outlays. For the purpose of enforcing the discretionary caps, the security category comprises discretionary appropriations for the Department of Defense, the Department of Homeland Security, the Department of Veterans

Affairs, the National Nuclear Security Administration, the intelligence community management account (95-0401-0-1-054), and discretionary accounts in budget function 150 (international affairs). The nonsecurity category comprises all discretionary appropriations not included in the security category.

[14] That reduction in interest on the public debt is projected using CBO's August 2011 forecast for interest rates. Those rates are lower than ones forecast earlier in the year and used in Congressional Budget Office, letter to the Honorable John A. Boehner and the Honorable Harry Reid estimating the impact on the deficit of the Budget Control Act of 2011.

[15] Discretionary spending refers to outlays from budget authority that is provided and controlled by appropriation acts. Mandatory spending refers to outlays from budget authority provided by laws other than appropriation acts.

[16] Budgetary resources consist of all sources of authority provided to federal agencies that permit them to incur financial obligations, including new budget authority, unobligated balances, direct spending authority, and obligation limitations.

[17] The Budget Control Act specifies that 18 percent of the $1.2 trillion goal for deficit reduction be assumed to result from debt-service savings; that amount comes to $216 billion. However, CBO estimates that the automatic spending reductions would produce debt-service savings of $169 billion through 2021.

[18] For further details, see Congressional Budget Office, *Estimated Impact of Automatic Budget Enforcement Procedures Specified in the Budget Control Act* (September 2011).

[19] See Congressional Budget Office, *CBO's 2011 Long-Term Budget Outlook* (June 2011).

[20] See Congressional Budget Office, *Federal Debt and the Risk of a Fiscal Crisis,* Issue Brief (July 2010).

[21] CBO estimated the magnitude of those effects for the paths of federal debt presented in *CBO's 2011 Long-Term Budget Outlook*. CBO estimated that under the extended-baseline scenario in that report, real gross national product (GNP) would be reduced slightly by 2025 and by as much as 2 percent by 2035, compared with what it would be under the stable economic environment underlying most of the projections in that report. In addition, CBO estimated that under the alternative fiscal scenario in that report, real GNP would be 2 percent to 6 percent lower in 2025, and 7 percent to 18 percent lower in 2035, than under a stable economic environment. (GNP differs from GDP primarily by including the capital income that residents earn from investments abroad and excluding the capital income that nonresidents earn from domestic investment. In the context of analyzing the impact of growing deficits and debt, GNP is a better measure because projected budget deficits would be partly financed by inflows of capital from other countries.)

[22] See Congressional Budget Office, *Economic Impacts of Waiting to Resolve the Long-Term Budget Imbalance*, Issue Brief (December 2010).

[23] See Congressional Budget Office, *Estimated Impact of the American Recovery and Reinvestment Act on Employment and Economic Output from March 2011 Through June 2011* (August 2011) and Statement of Douglas W. Elmendorf, Director, Congressional Budget Office, before the Senate Committee on the Budget, *The Economic Outlook and Fiscal Policy Choices* (September 28, 2010).

[24] See Congressional Budget Office, *The Macroeconomic and Budgetary Effects of an Illustrative Policy for Reducing the Federal Budget Deficit* (July 2011).

[25] CBO's analysis considered a range of possible short-term effects on output. The medium-sized response reflected the assumption that each one-dollar reduction in the deficit would cause economic output to decline by a dollar in the short term, excluding the effects from changes in interest rates. At one end of the range, each one-dollar cut in the deficit was assumed to

cause cumulative economic output to decline by $0.60 over several quarters. At the opposite end of the range, each one-dollar cut in the deficit was assumed to cause economic output to decline by a cumulative $1.40. The dollar-for-dollar response lies within the ranges of estimated effects on economic output for many policies examined in CBO's analysis of the macroeconomic effects of ARRA.

[26] To illustrate a range of possible effects, CBO assumed that each dollar of deficit reduction would increase domestic investment by 20, 36, or 50 cents (reflecting different assumptions about the effects of deficits on both national saving and net borrowing from abroad).

[27] See Congressional Budget Office, *The Budget and Economic Outlook: An Update* (August 2011), Table 2-2. To reflect the high degree of uncertainty that accompanies estimates of the economic impact of fiscal policy, CBO used a range of assumptions about the extent to which changes in taxes and government spending affect the demand for goods and services, budget deficits affect private investment, and changes in marginal tax rates on labor income affect the labor supply. For more information about CBO's assumptions, see Congressional Budget Office, *The Macroeconomic and Budgetary Effects of an Illustrative Policy for Reducing the Federal Budget Deficit*.

[28] For further discussion, see Congressional Budget Office, *Policies for Increasing Economic Growth and Employment in 2010 and 2011* (January 2010) and Statement of Douglas W. Elmendorf, Director, Congressional Budget Office, before the Senate Committee on the Budget, *The Economic Outlook and Fiscal Policy Choices*.

[29] For numerous options for changing tax and spending policies, and estimates of their potential budgetary impacts, see Congressional Budget Office, *Reducing the Deficit: Spending and Revenue Options* (March 2011).

[30] For additional information on these topics, see Statement of Douglas W. Elmendorf, Director, Congressional Budget Office, before the Senate Committee on Finance, *Trends in Federal Tax Revenues and Rates* (December 2, 2010); and Congressional Budget Office, *An Analysis of the President's Budgetary Proposals for Fiscal Year 2012*.

[31] See Congressional Budget Office, *Policies for Increasing Economic Growth and Employment in 2010 and 2011* and Statement of Douglas W. Elmendorf, Director, Congressional Budget Office, before the Senate Committee on the Budget, *The Economic Outlook and Fiscal Policy Choices*.

[32] The effective marginal tax rate on capital income is the rate that would apply to the return on additional investment. That rate is averaged across all the businesses, people, and institutions that would receive that investment income (and that could face different tax rates).

[33] Reductions in saving can, in turn, affect labor supply. A smaller capital stock would lead to lower pretax wage rates, which would weaken people's incentives to work.

In: Federal Deficit Reduction ISBN: 978-1-62417-779-8
Editors: Carl Frankel and Dan Iglehart

Chapter 3

REDUCING THE BUDGET DEFICIT: POLICY ISSUES*

Marc Labonte

SUMMARY

In 2009, the federal budget deficit (the difference between outlays and revenues) exceeded $1 trillion for the first time, and it has remained above $1 trillion since. Those years also marked the largest the deficit has been as a share of gross domestic product (GDP) in the period since World War II. The budget is not projected to be on a sustainable path under current policy, in the sense that it leads the publicly held debt to continuously grow more quickly than GDP. The timing of deficit reduction remains a difficult issue because of continued weakness in the economy.

If deficits are reduced too quickly, the economy might tip back into recession. If unsustainable deficits persist for too long in the economic recovery, it could crowd out private investment and, in the worst case scenario, investors could refuse to continue to finance deficits that they believed were unsustainable.

As one example of the policy changes that would return the budget to a sustainable path, the Congressional Research Service (CRS) estimates that stabilizing debt as a share of GDP at its 2011 level would require

---

* This is an edited, reformatted and augmented version of a Congressional Research Service publication, CRS Report for Congress R41778, from www.crs.gov, prepared for Members and Committees of Congress, dated February 15, 2012.

budget deficits averaging 2.8% of GDP over the next 10 years. In dollar terms, the deficit could equal $200 billion in 2013, rising to more than $600 billion from 2015 on.

Under the Congressional Budget Office's (CBO's) current law baseline, the deficit is already on a sustainable path. Under CBO's Alternative Fiscal Scenario, which modifies the current law baseline by assuming that expiring tax provisions and the "doc fix" to Medicare are extended and that the future automatic spending cuts under the Budget Control Act (BCA) do not come into effect, the deficit would decline from more than 9% of GDP in 2011 to 5% of GDP in 2015, then rise to 6% of GDP by 2022. To reduce the deficit to sustainable levels under this scenario would require some combination of spending cuts and tax increases equivalent to roughly $800 billion in 2013, falling to $275 billion in 2015, then rising to $900 billion by 2022.

The recent growth in deficits is the result of spending reaching its highest level as a share of GDP since 1945 and revenues reaching their lowest level as a share of GDP since 1950. Revenues were low because of the recession and because of the temporary extension of expiring tax provisions, such as the "alternative minimum tax (AMT) patch" and "Bush tax cuts."

If these tax cuts are extended again, revenues are estimated to be reduced by about 2.5% of GDP from 2014 on and will remain around their historical average from 2015 on.

Thus far, policy changes to reduce the deficit have targeted mainly discretionary spending. The BCA would reduce discretionary spending by $1.5 trillion and mandatory spending by less than $0.2 trillion over 10 years if automatic cuts are allowed to begin in 2013. Including interest savings, the BCA would reduce the deficit by about 1% of GDP from 2014 on.

Even if these cuts proceed as scheduled, overall spending is projected to rise and remain above its historical average over the next 10 years because of the growth in mandatory spending. Defense, Social Security, and Medicare account for more than half of total spending. Outside of those three programs and net interest, all other spending is about three-quarters the size of the budget deficit in 2012.

Growth in entitlement spending on the elderly drives long-term projections of large budget deficits—by mid-century, outlays on Social Security and health programs would exceed total revenues. Most proposals to reform entitlement programs for the elderly would generate significant budgetary savings in the long run, but little budgetary savings in the short run, partly because most proposals exempt current retirees from reform and partly because the savings from these changes would compound over time.

The US fiscal outlook is not a purely long-term issue, however—deficits are already at unsustainably high levels today.

INTRODUCTION

The federal budget has been in deficit (i.e., spending has exceeded revenues) since 2002, and deficits became significantly larger in 2009. That year, the deficit topped $1 trillion for the first time ever, and it is projected to remain above $1 trillion in 2012 for the fourth year in a row.[1] Relative to the overall size of the economy, budget deficits from 2009 to 2011 have been significantly larger than in any other year since World War II.

From 1946 to 2008, budget deficits averaged 1.7% of gross domestic product (GDP) and exceeded 5% of GDP only three times (equaling 7.2% in 1946, 6.0% in 1983, and 5.1% of GDP in 1985). From 2009 to 2011, the budget deficit averaged 9.3% of GDP, and it is projected to equal 7% of GDP in 2012.[2] Current deficits are larger as a share of GDP than any recorded historically except for those recorded during the Civil War, World War I, and World War II. In the past, deficits have proven sustainable because periods of moderate growth in the debt relative to GDP have been followed by periods when debt fell relative to GDP. Under current policy, deficits are projected to cause the federal debt to continuously grow faster than national income, which is unsustainable. The federal debt held by the public has grown from 40% of GDP in 2008 to a projected 73% of GDP in 2012.

Congress has expressed interest in examining policy options to reduce the deficit. The Congressional Research Service (CRS) does not take a position on the best way to reduce the deficit. This report organizes and presents information to help policymakers frame the debate. This report first discusses the size of projected budget deficits, then discusses how much the deficit would need to be reduced to return to long-term sustainability, then analyzes alternative time frames for reducing the deficit, and finally discusses broad policy choices for reducing the deficit.

WHAT POLICY CHANGES HAVE BEEN TAKEN TO REDUCE THE DEFICIT SO FAR?

From FY2001 to FY2010, policy changes added to budget deficits each year.[3] In FY2011, policy changes were a mix of deficit-reducing legislation and deficit-increasing legislation. To date, recent policy steps to reduce the deficit have primarily focused on reducing discretionary spending (i.e., spending that is provided and controlled through the appropriations process).

Discretionary outlays declined from $1.347 trillion in 2010 and $1.346 trillion in 2011 to a projected $1.308 trillion in 2012. Part of that decline is caused by a decline in spending on overseas contingency operations (OCO), but most is the result of a decline in non-defense discretionary spending. Because inflation reduces the purchasing power of $1 over time, the decline is larger in real terms. Relative to the January 2011 baseline level, which adjusts for inflation, discretionary spending was reduced by $29 billion in 2011.[4]

The reduction in 2011 discretionary spending occurred through the 2011 appropriations process. For 2012 to 2021, the Budget Control Act (P.L. 112-25) reduced discretionary spending and mandatory spending were reduced relative to the baseline.[5] The Budget Control Act cut spending through a two-step process.[6] In the first step, student loan programs were cut and statutory caps were set for discretionary spending for 2012 to 2021, with OCO, disaster spending, and emergency spending exempt from the caps. In the second round (often referred to as the “trigger”), additional spending cuts will be implemented beginning in January 2013. Most of these round two spending cuts will fall on discretionary spending, through sequestration (the across-the-board cancellation of budgetary resources) in 2013 and a reduction to the statutory discretionary caps for 2014 to 2021. Most mandatory programs are exempted from the act’s cuts, but a few smaller programs and parts of Medicare that are not will be cut through a sequestration from 2013 to 2021. The cut to Medicare is capped at 2%.

Relative to 2011 levels adjusted for inflation, CBO projects that the Budget Control Act reduces defense discretionary spending by $15 billion in 2012 and $812 billion over 10 years and nondefense discretionary spending by $12 billion in 2012 and $714 billion over 10 years.[7] These estimates require some assumption to be made about the levels of discretionary spending that will occur in categories that are exempt from the caps. For example, CBO assumes that emergency spending, which is exempted from the caps and designated by Congress and the President, will be zero in the next 10 years; if emergency spending does take place, discretionary savings from the Budget Control Act would be reduced dollar for dollar. In addition, the Budget Control Act cuts mandatory spending on student loan programs by $5 billion over 10 years and cuts other mandatory spending (mostly Medicare) through the second-round sequester by $165 billion over 9 years.[8] Since lower outlays would result in a lower debt relative to the baseline, debt service savings from these spending cuts would reduce the deficit by roughly another $300 billion over 10 years. Including these interest savings, the Budget Control Act reduces the annual deficit by about 1% of GDP from 2014 on.

If Congress acts to prevent the second round of spending cuts from taking place beginning in January 2013, but leaves the first round discretionary caps in place, total discretionary spending would be reduced by $778 billion over 10 years. In this scenario, mandatory spending would be cut by only $5 billion, with the cuts falling on student loan programs.

Although spending has been cut, other policy goals, such as stimulating the economy, have also led to recent policy changes that have increased the deficit relative to the baseline. For example, CBO estimates that the Tax Relief, Unemployment Insurance Reauthorization, and Job Creation Act of 2010 (P.L. 111-312) increased the deficit by $374 billion in 2011, of which $204 billion is attributable to the extension of expiring tax provisions. This act extended the "Bush tax cuts" [9] for two years, extended the alternative minimum tax (AMT) "patch" for one year,[10] extended and expanded unemployment benefits for one year, and implemented a one year payroll tax cut. The 112th Congress has debated whether each of these provisions should be allowed to expire as scheduled or extended further and whether further extensions should be deficit-financed or offset by spending cuts or other tax increases.

HOW LARGE ARE PROJECTED DEFICITS UNDER CURRENT POLICY?

Absent policy changes, budget deficits would change over time because spending and revenue levels automatically change over time. Baseline budget projections are used to provide a benchmark against which budgetary decisions can be made and policy proposals can be compared over the budget window. A baseline is not meant to be the best guess of future outcomes or the most desirable outcome, but a reasonable starting point for comparing policy options. The projected magnitude and path of budget deficits depends greatly on what baseline assumptions are made.

CBO estimates an official 10-year *current law* baseline, which assumes that certain provisions of law will expire as scheduled, even though many of these provisions have routinely been extended in the past.[11] Examples of such provisions include the 2001 and 2003 tax cuts (popularly known as the "Bush tax cuts"), which were extended until the end of 2012 to avoid their expiration at the end of 2010, and the "alternative minimum tax (AMT) patch," which has been repeatedly extended, most recently until the end of 2011. Another example is the Medicare cuts required in law by the sustainable growth physician payment formula; Congress has enacted legislative overrides to prevent those cuts (popularly known as the "doc fix") each year since 2003.[12] CBO's current law baseline also assumes that the second round of spending cuts under the Budget Control Act will occur in 2013 as scheduled. Under the current law baseline, the deficit would decline to about 1% of GDP by 2017, mostly due to the baseline assumptions that the Bush tax cuts and AMT patch will be allowed to expire as scheduled.

CBO also presents an unofficial Alternative Fiscal Scenario, which is a *current policy* baseline that assumes that spending and revenue policies in place now would remain in place. The Alternative Fiscal Scenario modifies the current law baseline by assuming that the doc fix[13] and all expiring tax provisions are extended (including the Bush tax cuts and the AMT patch, as well as dozens of smaller "extenders," with the exception of the payroll tax cut). It also assumes that the second round spending cuts in the Budget Control Act "trigger" will not come into effect in 2013 as scheduled, although it assumes that the first round discretionary caps will remain in place. It yields much larger budget deficits, because the policy changes raise outlays or lower revenues and because the larger budget deficits increase the interest that must be paid on the national debt.

Table 1 illustrates deficit projections under various scenarios, starting with the current law baseline and ending with the Alternative Fiscal Scenario. Under the Alternative Fiscal Scenario, the deficit would bottom out at 5.1% of GDP in 2015. It would then begin to rise again, and reach 6.1% of GDP by the end of the projection window. From 2017 on, the deficit under the Alternative Fiscal Scenario is more than four times larger than the current law baseline relative to GDP. The extension of the Bush tax cuts and AMT patch adds $5.4 trillion to the deficit over 10 years, more than the effects of all of the other assumptions made in the Alternative Fiscal Scenario combined.[14]

Discretionary spending poses conceptual problems for baseline projections. Baseline projections are attempting to extrapolate current policy, not predict the most likely outcome. Because it is determined on an annual basis, there is more than one reasonable assumption of what could be considered an extension of "current policy" into the future. In its baseline projection, CBO assumes that discretionary spending will match the levels set by the Budget Control Act. But the Budget Control Act only sets certain types of discretionary spending in statute; it sets no limit on overseas contingency operations (OCO) or any emergency spending, as designated by Congress and the President.

Table 1. Deficit Projections Under Alternative Assumptions
Fiscal Year

	2012	2013	2014	2016	2017	2018	2019	2020	2021	2022	
				billions of dollars							
CBO Current Law	$1,079	$585	**$345**	$269	$302	$220	$196	$258	$280	$279	$339
Baseline											
Baseline + "Doc Fix"	$1,088	$604	$366	$293	$330	$252	$233	$301	$330	$334	$401
Baseline + "Doc Fix" +	$1,100	$683	$483	$399	$427	$346	$328	$398	$432	$443	$518
Extenders											
Baseline + "Doc Fix" +	$1,111	$916	$822	$794	$869	$841	$880	$1,014	$1,117	$1,201	$1,357
Extenders + Extend											
"Bush Tax Cuts" and											
"AMT Patch"											
CBO Alternative Fiscal	$1,111	$981	$917	$899	$981	$960	$1,005	$1,144	$1,253	$1,344	$1,495
Scenario											
				% of GDP							
CBO Current Law	7.0%	3.7%	2.1%	1.5%	1.6%	1.1%	0.9%	1.2%	1.2%	1.2%	1.4%
Baseline											
Baseline + "Doc Fix"	7.0%	3.8%	2.2%	1.7%	1.8%	1.3%	1.1%	1.4%	1.5%	1.4%	1.6%
Baseline + "Doc Fix" +	7.1%	4.3%	2.9%	2.3%	2.3%	1.8%	1.6%	1.8%	1.9%	1.9%	2.1%
Extenders											
Baseline + "Doc Fix" +	7.2%	5.8%	5.0%	4.5%	4.6%	4.3%	4.3%	4.7%	4.9%	5.1%	5.5%
Extenders + Extend											
"Bush Tax Cuts" and											

Table 1. (Continued)

	2012	2013	2014	2016	2017	2018	2019	2020	2021	2022	
				billions of dollars							
"AMT Patch"											
CBO Alternative Fiscal	7.2%	6.2%	5.5%	5.1%	5.2%	4.9%	4.9%	5.3%	5.5%	5.7%	6.1%
Scenario											

Source: CRS calculations based on CBO data.

Notes: Cost of alternative policy assumptions includes additional debt service generated by those assumptions.CBO Alternative Fiscal Scenario = Baseline + "Doc Fix" + Extenders + Extend "Bush Tax Cuts" and "AMT Patch" + BCA Trigger. See text for details.

In the baseline, CBO assumes that OCO spending will increase at the rate of inflation and emergency spending will be zero.[15] Altering those assumptions would result in higher or lower projections of baseline spending under current law. Prior to enactment of the Budget Control Act, CBO assumed that discretionary spending would increase at the rate of inflation (i.e., would stay constant in real terms)—an assumption that was lower than historical growth rates. Under this assumption, deficits would be nearly one percentage point of GDP larger by the end of the 10-year budget window.

Budget projections are subject to a high degree of uncertainty—based on history, actual outcomes are likely to be much better or worse than projections. OMB estimates that the absolute average errors for its budget deficit projections are 1.5% of GDP for the next budget year and 3.5% of GDP for five years in the future.[16] This implies that maintaining the status quo (under the "current policy" baseline) could lead to a successful return to sustainability in five years, or to sustainability problems that are more serious than current projections would suggest.

WHY ARE DEFICITS PROJECTED TO DECLINE?

As *Table 1* illustrates, much of the projected reduction in the deficit over the next 10 years is a function of the assumptions made by the current law baseline. But even the Alternative Fiscal Scenario projects that the deficit will fall from over 9% of GDP in 2009-2011 to 7% of GDP in 2012 to as low as 4.9% of GDP in 2017. The deficit declines under the Alternative Fiscal Scenario for the following reasons:

- CBO projects that revenues automatically rise and certain mandatory spending automatically falls as the economy eventually returns to full employment. Economists refer to these changes as "automatic stabilizers." Assuming all expiring tax provisions are extended, revenues are projected to rise from about 15% of GDP in 2011 to 18% of GDP from 2017 on.[17] By 2015, unemployment compensation is projected to fall to less than half of its 2011 level in nominal dollars, although this is partly due to the expected expiration of the temporary extension of benefits.
- The temporary spike in budget authority caused by the American Reinvestment and Recovery Act (ARRA, P.L. 111-5, popularly known as the 2009 "Economic Stimulus Act") has dissipated. ARRA

was intended to be only a temporary boost to spending to stimulate the economy, and Congress has allowed budget authority to return to close to pre-ARRA levels to date.[18]

- Most financial stabilization outlays in the federal budget occurred within the Troubled Asset Relief Program (TARP)[19] or on transfers to the government sponsored enterprises (GSEs). CBO projects that there will be only minimal outlays on financial stabilization programs going forward, due to improvements in financial markets and the expiration in 2010 of Treasury authority to enter into new contracts with regards to TARP and the GSEs. In 2009, outlays of $243 billion were recorded for TARP and the GSEs. In 2010 and 2011, transfers to the GSEs declined and, due to budgetary conventions, TARP recorded negative outlays that reduced the deficit.[20]
- CBO assumes in the Alternative Fiscal Scenario that discretionary spending will adhere to the first round discretionary caps created by the Budget Control Act. This would reduce discretionary spending from 9% of GDP in 2011 to 6% of GDP in 2022, which would be its lowest level since data were first collected in 1962.

The projected decline in deficits is temporary, under any scenario in *Table 1*, and is followed by a gradual, long-term increase in the projected deficit. Long-term projections indicate that budget deficits would eventually become very large relative to GDP outside the projection window under current policy if revenues remain similar to their historical share of GDP. Under a long-term projection of current policy, CBO projects deficits would exceed 10% of GDP by 2026 and 20% of GDP by 2043.[21]

HOW MUCH DEFICIT REDUCTION IS NECESSARY?

The targeted amount of deficit reduction depends on the policy goal. A balanced budget could be pursued so that the government would have a neutral effect on the national saving rate (by accounting identity, budget deficits reduce the national saving rate).[22] Since the United States has a low national saving rate relative to other countries and relative to domestic investment needs, a case could be made that the government should at least not continue to reduce the national saving rate by running budget deficits in the future. If the policy goal were for the government to increase the national saving rate or reduce the federal debt, then the government could target a budget surplus.

Some economists call for a balanced structural budget, which would allow for modest deficits in downturns and budget surpluses in boom times. For 2009 to 2011, a structurally balanced budget would have allowed for an actual deficit of about 21/4% of GDP.[23]

A less ambitious policy goal would be to return fiscal policy to a sustainable path. History demonstrates that budget deficits can be sustained indefinitely as long as they are small enough that government debt does not continuously grow more quickly than GDP. The budget is not projected to be on a sustainable path under current policy (as defined by the Alternative Fiscal Scenario) because the debt held by the public would continuously grow more quickly than GDP, reaching 94% of GDP in 2022, thus implying that an ever-growing portion of national income would be needed to meet interest payments. As long as investors remain willing to finance large deficits, there is no barrier to the debt continuing to grow relative to GDP, and there has been no difficulty in financing it to date. At some point, however, investors would refuse to continue to finance such deficits, because the proportion of national income devoted to interest payments cannot rise indefinitely.[24] The size of the deficit compatible with sustainability depends on the size of the debt at the time it is stabilized and projected GDP growth rates. Because it is unknown how much longer the debt can be increased relative to GDP, for illustrative purposes, CRS estimates the budget deficits that would be consistent with stabilizing debt as a share of GDP at its projected 2012 level (73% of GDP) based on CBO's projections of GDP growth. Stabilizing the debt at 2012 levels would require annual budget deficits no larger than approximately 1% of GDP in 2013, rising to 3.5% of GDP in 2015 and 2016, falling to 2.75% of GDP from 2019 on.[25] In dollar terms, this would amount to a deficit of about $175 billion in 2013, rising to the $600 billion range from 2015 on. If actual policy followed the current law baseline, the budget deficit is already projected to be on a sustainable path. Compared with the Alternative Fiscal Scenario in *Table 1*, achieving sustainability would require some combination of spending cuts and tax increases equivalent to roughly $800 billion in 2013, falling to $275 billion in 2015, and rising each year thereafter until it exceeds $900 billion by 2022. In other words, one possible path to fiscal sustainability is to allow the policy changes already scheduled in law to occur. Another possible path is to prevent those changes from occurring, and then make offsetting cuts in spending or increases in taxes of $800 billion in 2013. CRS makes no recommendations on the best set of policies to achieve sustainability.

Under CBO's Alternative Fiscal Scenario and current interest rate projections, net interest on the federal debt is larger than the sustainable budget deficit, meaning that revenues would need to exceed non-interest spending (what economists call a "primary surplus") to stabilize the debt relative to GDP. Were GDP growth lower or interest rates higher than projected, the primary surplus would have to be larger to be sustainable, and vice versa. By historical standards, CBO's projections of economic growth over the next 10 years are relatively modest, but this is mostly because CBO projects that the labor supply will grow much more slowly than it has historically due to the aging of the population. Projections assume that interest rates will remain at relatively low levels by historical standards over the next 10 years. CBO estimates that if interest rates rose to their average level from 1991 to 2000, the budget deficit would be an average of $100 billion higher per year over the next 10 years. If interest rates rose to their average level from 1981 to 1990, the budget deficit would be an average of $500 billion higher per year over the next 10 years.[26]

Because deficits are projected to continue to grow in the long run, growing cuts in spending or increases in taxes would be required over time to maintain sustainability. Larger cuts in spending or increases in taxes would be required today to spread those changes evenly over time. For example, CBO projects that spending would need to be cut or revenues increased by 8.3% of GDP immediately to stabilize the debt-to-GDP ratio over the next 75 years, which would result in a projected budget surplus in 2012.[27]

The US fiscal outlook is not a purely long-term issue, however—deficits are already at unsustainably high levels today, and while projected deficits are larger than today's deficits outside the 10-year budget window, they are also more uncertain. The deficit is a long-term issue in that the economic consequences from running large deficits have been minor to date, but there is the risk that that the deficit's effect on the economy could become negative, possibly acutely so, at any time. Deficits are also a long-term issue in the sense that most observers believe fundamental reforms to outlays and revenues would be necessary to put the budget on a sustainable path; however, any delay to implementing those changes increases the eventual budgetary cost of returning to a sustainable fiscal path, all else equal.

How Quickly Should the Deficit Be Reduced?

The state of the economy is an important factor to consider in determining the desired timing of deficit reduction. All else equal, mainstream economic theory predicts that reducing the deficit would have a contractionary effect on the economy in the short run, whether it be through tax increases or spending reductions. During a period of robust economic growth, that contractionary effect would be more easily absorbed by other sectors of the economy, and the expansion would likely be sustained. During a period of high unemployment, such as the present, reducing the budget deficit would be expected to make unemployment higher (or fall more slowly) than would otherwise be the case, all else equal. On these grounds, an argument could be made for postponing deficit reduction until the economy improves. Given that the effect on the economy is proportional to the size of the deficit reduction, avoiding unwanted contractionary effects also argues for a gradual approach to deficit reduction.

On the other hand, the risk of a fiscal crisis as long as the deficit is at an unsustainable level would argue for moving to sustainability as quickly as possible to eliminate that risk. Low interest rates indicate that markets believe there is little risk of a crisis currently, but market sentiment can change quickly, as has occurred in countries such as Greece and Ireland. In these countries, GDP has contracted deeply and unemployment has risen sharply.

CBO projects that unemployment will rise to 9% in 2013 and 2014. These economic projections are based on the CBO "current law" baseline deficit, which is reduced rapidly between 2012 and 2013. Under the Alternative Fiscal Scenario, which projects a more gradual reduction in the deficit, CBO projects that unemployment would be between 7.4% and 8.9% in 2013. Nevertheless, CBO projects that significant deficit reduction under the current law baseline would not prevent the eventual return to full employment by 2017.

POLICY OPTIONS FOR DEFICIT REDUCTION

Budget deficits can be reduced through cuts in spending, higher taxes, or a combination of both. Plans to reduce the deficit are faced with the fact that Social Security, Medicare, and defense make up more than half of total spending. *Figure 1* compares the projected deficit to overall spending and revenues in FY2012. It shows that the deficit is about three-quarters the size of all non-interest spending outside of Social Security, Medicare, and defense discretionary. It is also more than three-quarters of total discretionary spending (defense and non-defense combined). It is about half the size of total revenues.

Budget deficits are the result of the shortfall between spending and revenue. As seen in *Figure 2*, spending in 2009 reached its highest level as a share of GDP since 1945 and revenues have reached their lowest level as a share of GDP since 1950.

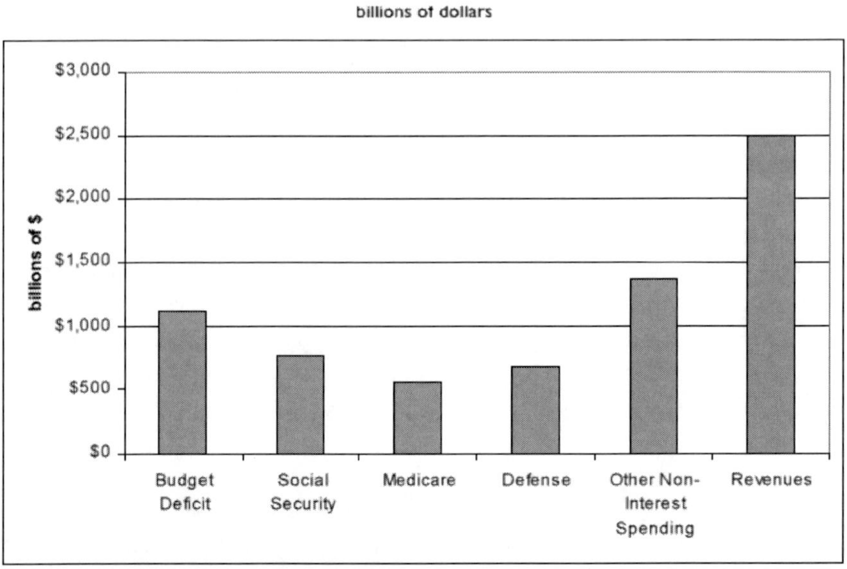

Source: CRS calculations based on CBO data.

Note: Budget deficit, spending, and revenues for 2012 are projected based on the January CBO baseline.

Figure 1. Selected Data from FY2012 Federal Budget.

From 1946 to 2008, outlays averaged 19.6% of GDP, and were generally below 20% of GDP until 1975, above 20% of GDP from 1975 to 1996, and below 20% of GDP from 1997 to 2005. From 2009 to 2011, outlays averaged 24.1% of GDP.

From 1946 to 2008, revenues averaged 17.8% of GDP, showing no long-term upward or downward trend from 1952 to 2007. Revenues were at least 17% of GDP in each year during that period except for 1955, 1959, 2003, and 2004, when they were between 16% and 17%. From 2009 to 2011, revenues were below 16%.

Just as recent deficits are the combination of all past outlay and revenue decisions, returning the budget to balance would be difficult without a combination of outlay and revenue changes.

For instance, to return the budget to balance while maintaining 2011 revenue levels would require that outlays decline to a share of GDP last seen in the 1950s.

Likewise, to balance the budget while maintaining 2011 outlay levels would require revenues to rise to their highest share of GDP ever.

1946-2022

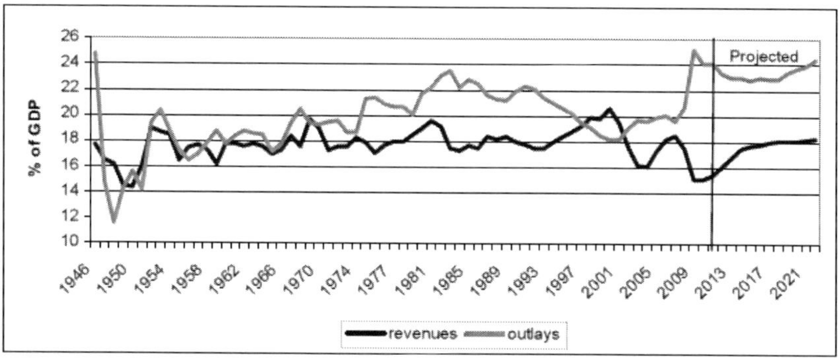

Source: OMB and CRS calculations based on CBO data.
Notes: See Table 1 for details on the Alternative Fiscal Scenario.

Figure 2. Federal Revenues and Outlays, Historical and Projected Under the Alternative Fiscal Scenario.

Federal Spending

Total spending under the Alternative Fiscal Scenario would fall by nearly one percentage point of GDP from 2011 to 2012, and is projected to average 23.4% of GDP in the 10-year budget window. (Total spending under the CBO current law baseline never falls below 21.5% of GDP.) From 1946 to 2008, there were only three years when outlays were above 23% of GDP. By 2022, total spending is projected to exceed its 2011 share of GDP under the Alternative Fiscal Scenario—despite discretionary spending falling to its lowest share of GDP since data was first collected—because mandatory spending and net interest on the federal debt grow relative to GDP. The projected increase in net interest is due to the growth in the federal debt and the return to more normal interest rates from the below-average rates currently prevailing.

Discretionary Spending

Large budget deficits relative to GDP since 2009 have corresponded with higher levels of discretionary spending relative to GDP, but not historically high levels since data was first available in 1962, as seen in *Figure 3*. Defense discretionary spending was higher from 1962 to 1992 as a share of GDP than it was in 2010. From 1963 to 2001, defense discretionary spending generally fell relative to GDP—but not in terms of nominal dollars. It then began to grow, when overseas military operations expanded. It currently remains well below the share of GDP that prevailed before the 1990s. Non-defense discretionary spending has shown no long-term upward or downward trend relative to GDP—except for an elevated period from 1975 to 1981, it has always stayed within 3.5% to 4.0% of GDP. Over the late 1990s, it fell to its lowest level of GDP since data has been collected, and then rose from that low base in the 2000s. It has been above its long-term average since 2009, but below the levels prevalent from 1975 to 1981. Since 2009, much of the growth in non-defense discretionary spending was a result of the 2009 Economic Stimulus Act. Most discretionary spending under this act will be completed by 2011.

1962-2022

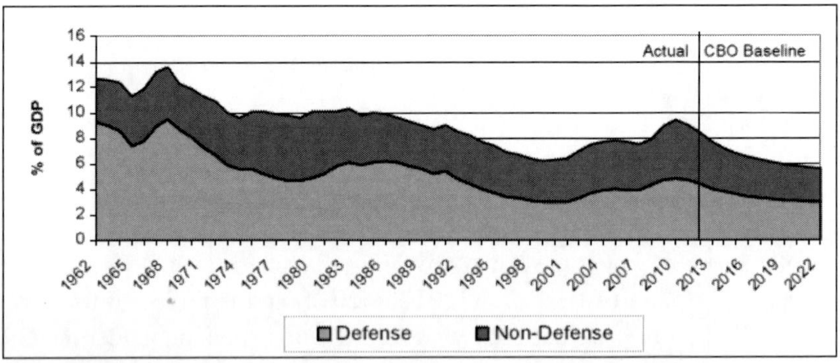

Source: OMB and CBO.

Note: Figure assumes that spending cuts under the Budget Control Act will occur as scheduled.

Figure 3. Discretionary Spending, Historical and Projected in the Baseline.

In the current law baseline, discretionary spending declines significantly relative to GDP over the next 10 years to its lowest share of GDP since data were first collected in 1962, as shown in *Figure 3*. The current law baseline assumes that discretionary spending will adhere to the levels set in the Budget Control Act. Even if the Budget Control Act's automatic "trigger" cuts are not implemented in 2013, total discretionary spending under the discretionary caps would still fall to its lowest share of GDP since 1962.

The CBO current law baseline assumes discretionary spending will fall in nominal terms (i.e., not adjusted for inflation) each year from 2011 to 2015. From 1963 to 2010, discretionary spending fell in nominal terms in only four years, most recently in 1996. Adjusted for inflation, the CBO baseline assumes that both defense and non-defense spending would fall in real terms each year from 2011 to 2022. If this occurred, it would mark a significant break from past policy, as shown in *Table 2*.

Table 2. Average Annual Real Growth Rates of Discretionary Spending Outlays. Actual and CBO Baseline, Adjusted for Inflation

	Defense	Non-Defense
2000-2008	5.1%	3.0%
2009-2010	5.7%	11.4%
2011-2022	-2.4%	-3.2%

Source: CRS calculations based on OMB and CBO data.

Notes: Data for 2000 to 2011 are actual; data for 2012 to 2022 assume that spending cuts under the Budget Control Act will occur as scheduled.

CBO includes the continuation of spending on overseas military operations at current levels (about $146 billion a year in 2012 dollars) in its baseline projection of discretionary spending throughout the 10-year budget window because it is exempt from the Budget Control Act caps. For defense, the timing and magnitude of any potential drawdown in overseas military operations could cause military spending to decline relative to the baseline, but traditionally such changes have not been motivated by deficit reduction. Even if current operations are reduced, future geopolitical events could require military personnel to be deployed elsewhere in the next 10 years, so the baseline does not necessarily overestimate future defense spending.

One macroeconomic implication of reducing discretionary spending is that most federal spending on physical capital (e.g., infrastructure) and human capital (e.g., education) is located in the discretionary portion of the budget. Economic theory predicts that a lower future capital stock would reduce the long-term size of the economy from what it otherwise would be, all else equal.[28]

In long-term projections, CBO holds discretionary spending constant as a share of GDP because it is determined annually. Because discretionary spending is held constant, it is not responsible for the growth of the budget deficit in long-term projections.

Mandatory Spending

Unlike discretionary spending, mandatory spending grew rapidly from 5% of GDP in 1962 to a range of 9% to 10.5% of GDP from 1975 to 2007, peaking in recession years because of automatic stabilizers. It exceeded 13%

of GDP from 2009 to 2011, marking its highest share of GDP since data were first compiled in 1962. In contrast to discretionary spending, mandatory spending is projected to continue to grow faster than inflation and exceed 13% of GDP over the next ten years under current policy. Since 1962, mandatory spending fell in nominal terms in only one year, 2010; if TARP and deposit insurance, which recorded negative outlays that year, are removed, all other mandatory spending grew in 2010.

Over the long term, the upward trend in mandatory spending in the past and future is dominated by Social Security, Medicare, and Medicaid, which accounted for about three-quarters of total mandatory spending in 2010. Between 2007 and the 2009 to 2011 period, the growth in mandatory spending was dominated by financial crisis programs, the 2009 Economic Stimulus Act spending, and automatic stabilizers (primarily located in the Income Security category).

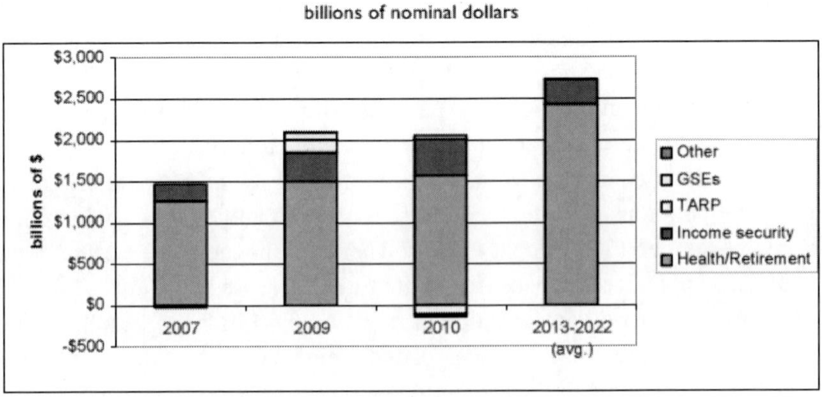

Source: CRS calculations based on CBO data.

Notes: Health/Retirement = Social Security, Medicare, Medicaid, Civil Service and Military Retirement, Veterans, and other health programs (net of offsetting receipts); GSEs = Government Sponsored Enterprises; TARP = Troubled Asset Relief Program; Income Security = unemployment benefits, means-tested transfer programs to households, refundable tax credits; Other = remaining programs net of offsetting receipts. Outlays can be negative for a category because offsetting receipts exceed spending or because of subsidy reestimates for credit programs. Totals for joint state-federal programs include only the federal share.

Figure 4. Mandatory Spending in Selected Years.

From 2007 to 2009, mandatory health and retirement programs (including Social Security, Medicare, and Medicaid) increased by $234 billion or 19%, as shown in *Figure 4.* Over the same period, income security outlays increased by $146 billion or 73%. In FY2009, TARP was created and the GSEs began to receive financial assistance, adding $152 billion and $91 billion to mandatory spending, respectively.

Outside of health and retirement programs, outlays on other mandatory programs are projected to decline significantly in nominal terms over the next 10 years. TARP registered negative outlays of $110 billion in 2010 and $37 billion in 2011, representing downward revisions of the previously estimated cost of the program, and is projected to record outlays of less than $1 billion per year over the next 10 years. Transfers to the GSEs declined to $5 billion in 2011, and are projected to average $3 billion per year over the next 10 years. As the economy improves, "automatic stabilizer" spending is also projected to decline: spending on income security programs more than doubled in nominal terms between 2007 and 2010, but is projected to decline from $438 billion in 2010 to an annual average of $302 billion over the next 10 years.

In long-term budget projections, rising budget deficits are driven primarily by the growth in entitlement programs for the elderly, particularly health spending. Social Security outlays are projected to rise from 4.8% of GDP today to 6.1% of GDP in 2035, and federal health outlays (mainly on Medicare and Medicaid) are projected to rise from 5.6% today to as much as 10.3% of GDP in 2035. By 2050, outlays on Social Security and health programs would exceed total revenues. In part, this growth is driven by the assumptions that go into these projections— revenues and discretionary spending are assumed to stay constant relative to GDP in the long run, whereas health spending per capita is projected to continue to grow faster than GDP per capita because it has historically grown much more quickly. If health spending per capita grew at the same rate as GDP per capita (technically, this is referred to as an excess cost growth rate of zero), much of the increase in federal spending would be avoided, although spending would still grow somewhat because of demographic changes—namely, the retirement of the baby boomers—that increased the number of recipients.[29]

The growth in elderly entitlement spending keeps deficits unsustainably large in the long run. Restraining the future growth rate of this spending would keep the deficit from growing, but it alone would not reduce the budget deficit in the short run. In effect, since the debt is already growing faster than GDP today, restraining elderly entitlement growth would keep the debt to GDP ratio on its current upward—and therefore, unsustainable—trajectory.[30] Most proposals to reform elderly entitlement programs would generate significant budgetary savings in the long run, but little budgetary savings in the short run, partly because most proposals exempt current retirees from reform and partly because the savings from these changes would compound over time. For example, immediately reducing excess cost growth for federal health spending to zero would reduce federal spending by 2% of GDP after 14 years, but by 0.7% of GDP after 5 years.[31]

Revenues

In 2009 and 2010, revenues were at historically low shares of GDP across all major categories— individual income taxes were at their lowest share of GDP since 1950, corporate income taxes were at their lowest share of GDP since the 1930s, social insurance receipts were at their lowest share of GDP since the 1970s, and excise taxes were at their lowest share of GDP since 1934, the first year for which data are available. In recent years, most revenues have come from the individual and social insurance categories. In 2011, income tax revenue rose as a share of GDP because of the economic recovery, but social insurance receipts declined as a share of GDP because of the payroll tax cut (P.L. 111-312), and total revenues remained below historical averages as a share of GDP. Revenues in the CBO "current law" baseline are projected to exceed 20% of GDP from 2015 on, which is higher than the historical average. This increase occurs primarily because CBO assumes that the "Bush tax cuts" and "AMT patch" expire as scheduled in current law. If the tax cuts and AMT patch continue to be extended (as assumed in the Alternative Fiscal Scenario), revenues would be about 2% of GDP lower in 2014, rising to 2.5% of GDP by 2021. In this scenario, total revenues would gradually increase relative to GDP over the next 10 years due to the improvement in the economy (initially) and "real bracket creep," returning to their historical average around 2014. Real bracket creep refers to the fact that the same tax structure generates more revenue relative to GDP when incomes rise. But revenues would not return to 18.5% of GDP, which is the highest share of GDP that revenues have reached since the Bush tax cuts were fully implemented, at any point in the next decade under the Alternative Fiscal Scenario because of the enactment of additional tax cuts since then. If policymakers decided to increase revenue to reduce the deficit, five broad choices are often discussed[32]:

- redesigning the structure of the tax system;
- adding new revenue sources, such as a carbon tax or a value added tax (VAT);

- increasing existing taxes;
- "broadening the tax base" by eliminating tax expenditures (deductions, exemptions, and credits); or
- allowing tax cuts to expire as scheduled.

Redesigning the tax system or adding new revenue sources could theoretically improve economic efficiency and might be more appealing to some than increasing existing taxes, but in practice, pressure to compensate those made worse off from these changes may result in those policies raising little additional revenue. Generally, economists favor eliminating tax expenditures over raising marginal tax rates on efficiency grounds, although some specific expenditures may promote economic efficiency. Tax expenditures have also been criticized on the grounds of equity and complexity.[33]

For long-term projections, defining revenues under current policy is problematic. Under current law, revenues are projected to gradually rise relative to GDP over the next 75 years because some parts of the tax system, notably the AMT, are not indexed for inflation and other parts of the system would experience "real bracket creep."[34] If current policy were instead considered to be defined as setting revenues at current levels or returned to historical levels, revenues would be insufficient to match the long-term growth in spending under current policy, and progressively larger budget deficits would result.

CONCLUSION

Budget deficits have reached historically high and unsustainable levels since 2009 because spending has been at its highest share of GDP since 1945 and revenues have reached their lowest share of GDP since 1950. By 2017, deficits decline to about 1% of GDP—a sustainable level in the sense that it would cause the federal debt to fall relative to GDP—under the official CBO "current law" baseline. This baseline makes several assumptions that would mark a significant change from current policy—that tax provisions such as the Bush tax cuts and AMT patch would be allowed to expire as scheduled although they have already been extended at least once, that cuts to Medicare physician payments would be allowed although Congress has routinely prevented those cuts, and that discretionary spending will fall to historically low shares of GDP under the Budget Control Act. Under CBO's Alternative Fiscal Scenario, budget deficits under a continuation of current policy (as opposed to current law) would remain between 5% and 6% of GDP and would continually rise as a share of GDP after 2014 over the next 10 years.

One policy goal is to place the deficit on a sustainable path so that the publicly held debt stabilizes as a share of GDP. For illustrative purposes, CRS estimates that to stabilize the debt as a share of GDP at its projected 2012 level (73% of GDP) would require average annual budget deficits of 2.8% of GDP over the next 10 years. In dollar terms, this would amount to a deficit of about $400 billion in 2012, rising to about $550 billion in 2015. Compared with the "current policy" baseline, this would require some combination of spending cuts and tax increases equivalent to more than $700 billion in 2012 and $400 billion in 2015.

Balancing the budget through changes to one subsection of the budget is not mathematically possible at 2012 levels. For example, total spending outside of Social Security, Medicare, defense, and net interest is projected to be roughly three-quarters the size of the budget deficit in 2012. Total revenues are projected to be about half the size of the deficit in 2012. To date, legislation to reduce the budget deficit has focused on reducing discretionary spending, but the budget deficit in 2012 is projected to be more than three quarters the size of total discretionary spending (defense and non-defense combined).

In long-term projections of current policy, unsustainable budget deficits are largely driven by the growth in elderly entitlement spending. By 2050, outlays on Social Security and health programs are projected to exceed total revenues. However, because deficits are already at unsustainable levels today, restraining the future growth rate of elderly entitlement spending alone would still leave an unsustainably large budget deficit—in effect, it would simply keep the deficit from getting larger. Most proposals to curb the future growth of these programs call for gradual changes that exempt those who are now elderly or near-elderly. These types of proposals typically result in modest deficit reduction in the short term.

The Budget Control Act is projected to reduce the deficit by about 1% of GDP on average over the next 10 years, mostly through discretionary spending cuts. If other current policies remain in place, this act would not appear to reduce the deficit enough to restore fiscal sustainability. In this scenario, revenues as a share of GDP will remain below their historical average and mandatory spending will remain at historically high levels as a share of GDP. Revenue levels are currently low because of the recession and tax cuts. The

Tax Relief, Unemployment Insurance Reauthorization, and Job Creation Act of 2010 further increased the deficit by an estimated $374 billion in 2011, of which $204 billion is attributable to the extension of expiring tax provisions.

End Notes

[1] All budget data presented in this report are from Congressional Budget Office, Preliminary Analysis of the President's Budget for FY2012, March 2011 and Congressional Budget Office, Budget and Economic Outlook, January 2012 (hereafter referred to as "CBO baseline"), or Office of Management and Budget, FY2013 Budget of the US Government, February 2012 (hereafter referred to as "President's Budget"). The budget deficit is the excess of outlays over revenues in a given year, broadly similar to the amount borrowed from the public that year. The publicly held debt is the accumulation of all past borrowing from the public. The gross debt is the publicly held debt and the intragovernmental debt (the debt that one part of the federal government borrows from another part, mainly government trust funds). All references to years are to fiscal years, unless otherwise noted. For background information on the debt and deficit, see CRS Report WKS0001_Overview, Federal Debt and Deficit: Key Sources, by Justin Murray.

[2] Expressing budget data as a percentage of GDP is most appropriate for making comparisons over extended periods of time because it allows the relative size of those amounts to be consistently compared. Dollar figures are not appropriate because of inflation, which means that a dollar has a smaller amount of purchasing power over time, and because as the economy has become larger, there are more resources available to finance spending through borrowing or taxes.

[3] For information on causes of the budget deficit, see CRS Report R41134, The Impact of Major Legislation on Budget Deficits: 2001 to 2010, by Marc Labonte and Margot L. Crandall-Hollick

[4] Although the FY2011 had already begun, appropriations had not been completed when the January baseline was released.

[5] For more information, see CRS Report R42013, The Budget Control Act of 2011: Effects on Spending Levels and the Budget Deficit, by Marc Labonte and Mindy R. Levit. All of the reductions in spending discussed here would lead to additional declines in spending on net interest because the federal debt would be lower than in the baseline.

[6] For more information, see CRS Report R41965, The Budget Control Act of 2011, by Bill Heniff Jr., Elizabeth Rybicki, and Shannon M. Mahan.

[7] Congressional Budget Office, Testimony Before the Joint Select Committee on Deficit Reduction, US Congress, October 26, 2011. The amount of savings garnered by the Budget Control Act depends on what baseline it is being compared with. For example, if it were being compared with a baseline based on 2010 levels of discretionary spending, the savings would be higher than if it were compared with 2010 levels.

[8] Congressional Budget Office, Budget and Economic Outlook, January 2012, p. 13.

[9] The Economic Growth and Tax Relief Reconciliation Act of 2001 (EGTRRA; P.L. 107-16) and the Jobs and Growth Tax Relief Reconciliation Act of 2003 (JGTRRA; P.L. 108-27) are popularly referred to as the "Bush tax cuts." Various acts since then have sped up the implementation or prevented the expiration of certain provisions of those acts.

[10] The alternative minimum tax is not adjusted for inflation. As a result, Congress has enacted a series of temporary "patches" to prevent a spike in taxpayers subject to the AMT. See CRS Report RL30149, The Alternative Minimum Tax for Individuals, by Steven Maguire.

[11] Some expiring mandatory spending programs are assumed to continue under the baseline. According to CBO, "The Deficit Control Act specifies some exceptions. For example, spending programs whose authorizations are set to expire are assumed to continue if they have outlays of more than $50 million in the current year and were established at the time of or before the enactment of the Balanced Budget Act of 1997. Programs established after that law was enacted are not automatically assumed to continue but are considered individually in consultation with the budget committees." Congressional Budget Office, Budget and Economic Outlook, January 2012, p. 11. For a list of programs that CBO assumes will expire in its baseline, see Congressional Budget Office, Budget and Economic Outlook, January 2012, Table 3.3.

[12] For more information, see CRS Report R40907, Medicare Physician Payment Updates and the Sustainable Growth Rate (SGR) System, by Jim Hahn and Janemarie Mulvey.

[13] The doc fix is the only expiring mandatory provision that CBO assumes will be continued in its Alternative Fiscal Scenario that is not also included in the current law baseline.

[14] The budgetary effects of extending the AMT patch and Bush tax cuts cannot be separated because of an interactive effect that makes the cost of jointly extending them greater than the cost of extending them separately.

[15] Baseline spending levels for disasters and overseas military operations can be sensitive to the timing of appropriations acts. From the perspective of crafting a deficit reduction proposal, if one believes that a policy included in the baseline is unrealistic, such as a reduction in overseas contingency operations or the omission of future spending in response to an unforeseen emergency in the next 10 years, it can be included in a budget proposal rather than altering the baseline. The adjusted baseline in the President's budget includes a placeholder for future disasters equal to $80 billion over 10 years.

[16] Office of Management and Budget, FY2012 Budget of the US Government, Analytical Perspectives, February 2011, p. 471.

[17] Revenues also rise relative to GDP automatically over time because of "real bracket creep," meaning that the same tax system yields more revenue as national income rises.

[18] In 2008, before ARRA was enacted, non-defense discretionary budget authority was $494 billion. In 2009, it was $803 billion, but in 2011, it was $511 billion.

[19] TARP was created by the Emergency Economic Stabilization Act (P.L. 110-343).

[20] Reductions in TARP's projected lifetime cost led to negative outlays in 2010 and 2011 to compensate for what proved in hindsight to be too large an estimate of its cost in 2009.

[21] Long-term budget data can be found in Congressional Budget Office, The Long-Term Budget Outlook, June 2011. The figures cited here are under CBO's "alternative fiscal scenario." For more information, see CRS Report RL32747, The Economic Implications of the Long-Term Federal Budget Outlook, by Marc Labonte.

[22] In simple terms, saving is measured by the excess of income over spending. When the government's outlays exceed its revenues, it must borrow from the public to finance the difference, and it has a negative saving rate.

[23] Congressional Budget Office, The Budget and Economic Outlook, January 2012, Table C-2.

[24] Economic effects of an unsustainable budget deficit are discussed in CRS Report R40770, The Sustainability of the Federal Budget Deficit: Market Confidence and Economic Effects, by Marc Labonte.

[25] The sustainable deficit is significantly smaller in 2013 than later years because CBO projects low nominal GDP growth in 2013.

[26] Congressional Budget Office, Letter to the Honorable Paul Ryan, February 24, 2011, Table 2.

[27] Congressional Budget Office, The Long-Term Budget Outlook, June 2011, p. 15. Economists call this concept the "fiscal gap."

[28] About half of federal spending on physical capital is for defense, and reduced defense capital spending may not have the same economic effects as reduced non-defense capital spending.

[29] For more information, see CRS Report RL32747, The Economic Implications of the Long-Term Federal Budget Outlook, by Marc Labonte.

[30] This would be the case under the assumptions that discretionary spending and revenues stay around the historical average, as opposed to revenues being determined by current law.

[31] Congressional Budget Office, Long-Term Budget Outlook, June 2011, Figure 3-4.

[32] For a further analysis, see CRS Report R41641, Reducing the Budget Deficit: Tax Policy Options, by Molly F. Sherlock.

[33] For more information, see CRS Report RL33641, Tax Expenditures: Trends and Critiques, by Thomas L. Hungerford.

[34] The reason regular AMT "patches" have been enacted in recent years is to prevent an increase in taxpayers subject to the AMT due to inflation.

In: Federal Deficit Reduction ISBN: 978-1-62417-779-8
Editors: Carl Frankel and Dan Iglehart

Chapter 4

ECONOMIC EFFECTS OF POLICIES CONTRIBUTING TO FISCAL TIGHTENING IN 2013*

Benjamin Page and Felix Reichling

INTRODUCTION

Substantial changes to tax and spending policies are scheduled to take effect in January 2013, significantly reducing the federal budget deficit. According to the Congressional Budget Office's (CBO's) projections, if all of that fiscal tightening occurs, real (inflation-adjusted) gross domestic product (GDP) will drop by 0.5 percent in 2013 (as measured by the change from the fourth quarter of 2012 to the fourth quarter of 2013)—reflecting a decline in the first half of the year and renewed growth at a modest pace later in the year.[1] That contraction of the economy will cause employment to decline and the unemployment rate to rise to 9.1 percent in the fourth quarter of 2013. After next year, by the agency's estimates, economic growth will pick up, and the labor market will strengthen, returning output to its potential level (reflecting a high rate of use of labor and capital) and shrinking the unemployment rate to 5.5 percent by 2018.

---

* This is an edited, reformatted and augmented version of Congressional Budget Office report, Publication No. 4570, dated November 2012.

Output would be greater and unemployment lower in the next few years if some or all of the fiscal tightening scheduled under current law—sometimes called the fiscal cliff—was removed. However, CBO expects that even if all of the fiscal tightening was eliminated, the economy would remain below its potential and the unemployment rate would remain higher than usual for some time. Moreover, if the fiscal tightening was removed and the policies that are currently in effect were kept in place indefinitely, a continued surge in federal debt during the rest of this decade and beyond would raise the risk of a fiscal crisis (in which the government would lose the ability to borrow money at affordable interest rates) and would eventually reduce the nation's output and income below what would occur if the fiscal tightening was allowed to take place as currently set by law.

In August, CBO presented estimates of the budgetary and economic outcomes that would occur under current law and under an "alternative fiscal scenario" that represents a continuation of many long-standing policies and thus a significant reduction in the amount of fiscal tightening next year. To provide additional information about the sources of that tightening and its effects, this report presents estimates of the budgetary and economic impact of the main changes to current law that would occur under that alternative scenario, as well as estimates of the impact of eliminating various other components of fiscal tightening scheduled for 2013.

In order to focus on the short-term impact of policy decisions, the analysis in this report is based on the assumption that the fiscal tightening would be removed and current policies maintained for two years and that the tightening provided by current law would occur thereafter. (In contrast, CBO's August analysis of the alternative fiscal scenario was based on the assumption that those current policies would be maintained indefinitely.)

On the basis of its analysis, CBO concludes the following:

- Eliminating the automatic enforcement procedures established by the Budget Control Act of 2011 that are scheduled to reduce both discretionary and mandatory spending starting in January and maintaining Medicare's payment rates for physicians' services at the current level would boost real GDP by *about three-quarters of a percent* by the end of 2013 (see Figure 1).[2]
- Extending all expiring tax provisions other than the cut in the payroll tax that has been in effect since January 2011—that is, extending the tax reductions originally enacted in 2001, 2003, and 2009 and extending all other expiring provisions, including those that expired at

the end of 2011, except for the payroll tax cut—and indexing the alternative minimum tax (AMT) for inflation beginning in 2012 would boost real GDP by *a little less than 11/2 percent* by the end of 2013.

- Making all of the changes described in the two preceding bullets—which captures all of the policies included in the first two years of CBO's alternative fiscal scenario—would boost real GDP by *about 21/4 percent* by the end of 2013 (as CBO estimated in August).[3] Thus, of the total difference in the projected growth of GDP next year under current law and under the alternative fiscal scenario, about two-thirds owes to changes in tax policies and about one-third owes to changes in spending policies.
- The estimated economic effect next year of those changes in spending is about half the estimated effect of extending the expiring tax provisions, even though the budgetary impact of the changes in spending is less than one-quarter of the impact of the changes in taxes. The larger "bang for the buck" next year of the spending policies under the alternative fiscal scenario occurs because, CBO expects, a significant part of the decrease in taxes (relative to those under current law) would be saved rather than spent.
- Extending all expiring tax provisions other than the cut in the payroll tax and indexing the AMT for inflation—except for allowing the expiration of lower tax rates on income above $250,000 for couples and $200,000 for single taxpayers—would boost real GDP by *about 11/4 percent* by the end of 2013. That effect is nearly as large as the effect of making all of those changes in law and extending the lower tax rates on higher incomes as well (which CBO estimates to be a little less than 11/2 percent, as noted above), primarily because the budgetary impact would be nearly as large (and secondarily because the extension of lower tax rates on higher incomes would have a relatively small effect on output per dollar of budgetary cost).
- Extending both the current 2 percentage-point cut in the payroll tax and emergency unemployment benefits—extensions that are not assumed in the alternative fiscal scenario—would boost real GDP by *about three-quarters of a percent* by the end of 2013. Making those changes along with making all of the changes in CBO's alternative fiscal scenario would boost real GDP by *about 3 percent* by the end of 2013.

CBO'S ANALYTICAL APPROACH

For each potential change in law discussed in this report, CBO used evidence from empirical studies and econometric models to estimate the impact on:

- Output next year—specifically, the effect on real GDP in the fourth quarter of 2013 and on average nominal GDP in 2013 per dollar of total budgetary cost (measured in terms of additional government spending or reduction in taxes)—and
- Employment next year—specifically, the effect on years of full-time-equivalent (FTE) employment in the fourth quarter of 2013 and on average FTE-years in 2013 per million dollars of total budgetary cost in that year.

Although the analysis here focuses on those two measures, other criteria are also important for evaluating fiscal policies. Those other criteria include the economic effects in later years, consistency with long-term fiscal objectives, the distributional consequences (that is, who bears the costs and receives the benefits), and the value to society of any added goods and services that would be produced in the short term.[4]

The approach adopted to estimate the short-term economic impact of alternative policies is similar to the method that CBO has used to assess the impact of the American Recovery and Reinvestment Act and the impact of various potential policies designed to increase output and employment.[5] The estimated effects on output of a given policy include both its direct and indirect effects. Direct effects consist of immediate effects on economic activity. For example, government purchases of goods and services directly elicit economic activity and thereby have a direct dollar-for-dollar impact on output. Indirect effects may enhance or offset the direct effects. For example, if the economy has idle resources, as it does now, government funding for projects can lead to the hiring of otherwise unemployed workers. The additional spending by those workers, who would have more income, would constitute a positive indirect effect. In contrast, a substantial increase in government spending financed by borrowing tends to drive up interest rates, which discourages spending on investment and on durable goods by raising the cost of borrowed funds.

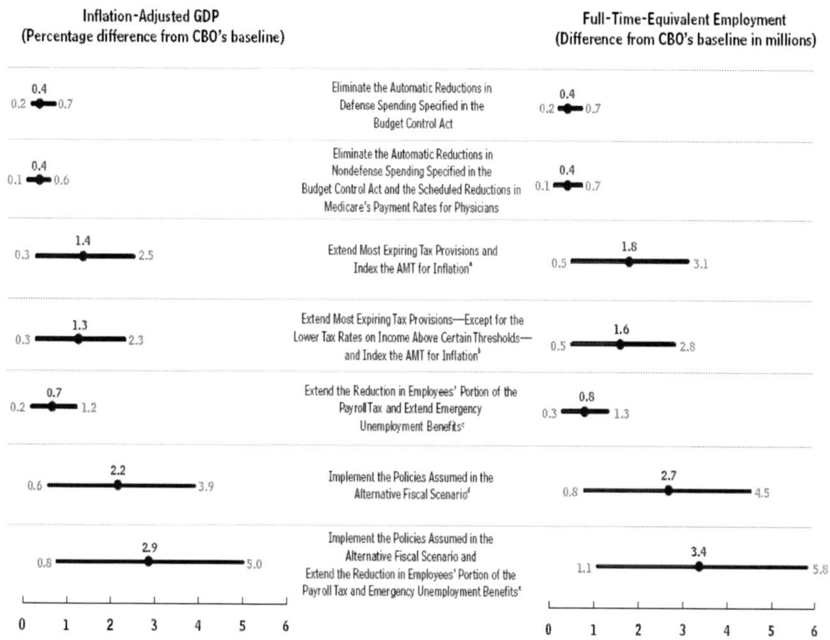

Source: Congressional Budget Office.

Notes: The estimated budgetary effects presented do not include debt service. GDP = gross domestic product; AMT = alternative minimum tax.

[a]This component incorporates extensions of title I of the Tax Relief, Unemployment Insurance Reauthorization, and Job Creation Act of 2010 (which extended for 2011 and 2012 income tax provisions enacted in 2001, 2003, and 2009); of title III of that act (which modified estate and gift taxation for 2010 through 2012); of the higher exemption amount for the AMT (which was previously increased through the end of December 2011), along with an indexing of higher exemption amount and AMT tax brackets for inflation after 2011; of the treatment of nonrefundable personal credits (which also was continued through the end of 2011); and of about 80 other tax provisions (many of which expired at the end of December 2011). Nearly all of those 80 provisions have been extended previously; some, such as the research and experimentation tax credit, have been extended more than once.

[b] This component incorporates extensions of title I of the Tax Relief, Unemployment Insurance Reauthorization, and Job Creation Act of 2010 (which extended for 2011 and 2012 income tax provisions enacted in 2001, 2003, and 2009) except for the reductions to the top two tax rates on ordinary income and to the tax rates on capital gains and dividends for taxpayers filing jointly with income above $250,000 and for single filers with income above $200,000 (with both thresholds indexed for inflation since 2009); of the elimination of limits on itemized deductions and personal exemptions except for those high-income taxpayers; of title III of that act (which modified estate and gift taxation for 2010 through 2012); and of about 80 other tax provisions (many of which expired at the end of December 2011). It also incorporates indexing the AMT for inflation.

[c] The budgetary cost is for a two-year extension of the policies.

[d] Implements the first two years of the alternative fiscal scenario, combining the first three components listed in the figure.

[e] Combines the first three components and the fifth component listed in the figure.

Figure 1. Estimated Economic Effects in the Fourth Quarter of 2013 of Eliminating Various Components of Fiscal Tightening Scheduled for Fiscal Years 2013 and 2014.

Those indirect "crowding-out" effects would offset some of the direct effects. In its analysis, CBO chose, on a judgmental basis, low and high estimates of the effects on output for a given policy to encompass most economists' views about the effects of that type of policy.

The monetary policy of the Federal Reserve has an important influence on the economic effects of changes in taxes and government spending. In its August 2012 *An Update to the Budget and Economic Outlook*, CBO anticipated that the economic slowdown brought about by fiscal tightening under current law, coupled with a lack of inflationary pressure, would prompt the Federal Reserve to introduce new policies to hold down the rate on 10-year Treasury notes. Changes in the laws governing federal taxes and spending that would offset the fiscal tightening scheduled under current law and ameliorate the projected economic slowdown could lead the Federal Reserve to scale back or eliminate those policies. In this analysis, CBO assumed that, at least through 2013, the Federal Reserve would react in that way. That reaction would increase long-term interest rates a little relative to the rates in CBO's baseline projections and thereby slightly attenuate the economic effects of policies that would reduce fiscal tightening.

Fiscal policies may also affect spending by individuals and businesses by altering people's uncertainty or confidence about future economic conditions or government policies. Many firms appear to be uncertain today about future demand for their products, and that uncertainty seems to be leading them to be cautious about increasing their investment and hiring. Fiscal policy actions that boosted demand might lessen that uncertainty and increase employment.[6] However, some fiscal policy actions might exacerbate uncertainty about future government policies—for example, if firms' managers wondered whether a temporary policy might later be extended or what other changes in fiscal policy might be made later. Because quantifying reactions of that sort to changes in fiscal policy would be extremely difficult, this report does not incorporate such reactions.

To assess a policy's impact on employment, CBO used a series of steps to translate the estimated effects on output into estimated effects on FTE-years (each FTE-year being 40 hours of employment per week for one year). First, CBO estimated the impact on the output gap—the percentage difference between actual output and potential output. Next, CBO calculated the magnitude and timing of effects of changes in the output gap on productivity, hours per worker, and employment using the historical relationships between those measures. Changes in the output gap affect employment gradually over several quarters, as part of a rise in output initially shows up as higher productivity and hours per worker rather than as increased employment. CBO also took account of the effect of changes in employment on the size of the labor force, because discouraged workers and people who have chosen to pursue activities such as schooling rather than work tend to return to the labor force when unemployment declines and the economic environment improves.

To measure the impact on employment in FTE-years, CBO incorporated the estimated effects of policies on the number of hours worked in addition to their effects on the number of people employed. Projected increases in the average number of people employed during a year do not include shifts from part-time to full-time work or overtime and are generally somewhat smaller than increases in FTE-years.

For estimates of the amounts in 2013 of additional output per dollar and employment per million dollars of total budgetary cost, the cost used in the calculations was the effect on the federal deficit in calendar year 2013. Policy options with a smaller impact per dollar require more budgetary resources to generate given amounts of extra output and employment, and those with a larger impact per dollar require less budgetary resources.[7]

Since its November 2011 analysis presented in *Policies for Increasing Economic Growth and Employment in 2012 and 2013*, CBO has refined some aspects of its analytic approach and its presentation of results. For example, CBO now estimates that changes in GDP affect employment more gradually than it estimated previously. That change implies that generating a given increase in employment in the first year of a policy requires a larger increase in GDP. In addition, CBO now presents the effects of different policies on nominal GDP per dollar of budgetary cost, whereas the previous analysis presented the effects on real GDP measured with 2008 prices; that change in presentation (which better matches the effect on GDP to the budgetary cost of a policy, measured in nominal dollars) has slightly increased the effects on output per dollar of budgetary cost presented in this report, while leaving the effects on employment unchanged.

Since its August 2012 analysis of the alternative fiscal scenario, CBO has made one change of note: To focus on the short-term impact of the policies that constitute that scenario and the others analyzed in this report, the current analysis is based on the assumption that the policies would be maintained though calendar year 2014 and that the changes embodied in current law would unfold thereafter. In contrast, the August analysis was based on the assumption that the polices would be maintained indefinitely. Shortening the duration of the policies significantly reduces their cumulative budgetary effects and therefore their drag on output and income in the long run.

However, that shorter duration makes little difference in the policies' projected budgetary and economic effects in the short run. In particular, because the tax cuts have been in place for so long, CBO expects that households would view an extension of current tax rates as a continuation of established tax policy and would therefore alter their spending very little. If households viewed the two-year extension as less than permanent, they might spend less and provide a smaller short-term boost to economic output. However, that effect might be offset by a positive effect from a smaller increase in long-term interest rates if participants in the financial markets felt less concerned about the prospect of higher government debt in the future.

SHORT-TERM EFFECTS OF POLICIES CONTRIBUTING TO FISCAL TIGHTENING

CBO estimated the short-term impact on output and employment of five sets of policies:

- Eliminate the scheduled automatic reductions in defense spending;
- Eliminate the scheduled automatic reductions in nondefense spending and the scheduled reductions in Medicare's payment rates for physicians;
- Extend most expiring tax provisions and index the AMT for inflation;
- Extend most expiring tax provisions—except for the lower tax rates on income above certain thresholds— and index the AMT for inflation; and
- Extend both the payroll tax cut and emergency unemployment benefits.

CBO also estimated the impact of two combinations of those sets of policies:

- The alternative fiscal scenario, which encompasses the first three items listed above, and
- The alternative fiscal scenario plus an extension of the payroll tax cut and emergency unemployment benefits (the first three items and the last one).

The effects of the policies differ both because they vary in their budgetary cost and because they spur output and employment by different amounts per dollar of budgetary cost.

Eliminate the Automatic Reductions in Defense Spending Specified in the Budget Control Act

The Budget Control Act specified automatic procedures to reduce both discretionary and mandatory spending during the coming decade in the event that specified amounts of deficit reduction were not achieved through legislation originating from a Congressionally appointed committee.[8] Those automatic reductions will take the form of equal cuts (in dollar terms) in funding for defense and nondefense programs in fiscal years 2013 through 2021. For 2013, those reductions will be achieved by automatically canceling a portion of the budgetary resources (in an action known as sequestration) for most discretionary programs as well as for some programs and activities that are financed by mandatory spending.[9] From 2014 to 2021, the reductions will be achieved by lowering the caps on discretionary budget authority as specified in the Budget Control Act and through sequestration for mandatory spending. The law exempts a significant portion of mandatory spending from sequestration, however.

CBO has previously estimated how much discretionary and mandatory funding will change under the automatic enforcement mechanisms, and those estimates are used in this analysis. However, the Administration's Office of Management and Budget would implement any reductions on the basis of its own estimates.[10]

CBO estimated in August that the automatic enforcement procedures will reduce outlays for defense programs by $24 billion in fiscal year 2013 and by $51 billion in fiscal year 2014 (see Table 1). Because mandatory spending makes up less than 1 percent of all defense spending, almost all of that reduction in outlays in the defense category will be achieved by sequestering discretionary budget authority provided for 2013 and by lowering the caps on defense appropriations in 2014.

CBO estimates that precluding those reductions in defense outlays would increase real GDP by 0.4 percent and increase full-time-equivalent employment by about 0.4 million in the fourth quarter of 2013 (see Figure 1 on page 3).

Table 1. Estimated Increase in the Deficit from Eliminating Various Components of Fiscal Tightening Scheduled for Fiscal Years 2013 and 2014 (Billions of dollars)

	2013	2014
Eliminate the Automatic Reductions in Defense Spending Specified in the Budget Control Act[a]	24	51
Eliminate the Automatic Reductions in Nondefense Spending Specified in the Budget Control Act and the Scheduled Reductions in Medicare's Payment Rates for Physicians[a]	40	61
Extend Most Expiring Tax Provisions and Index the AMT for Inflation[a,b]	330	420
Extend Most Expiring Tax Provisions—Except for the Lower Tax Rates on Income Above Certain Thresholds— and Index the AMT for Inlation[a,c]	288	382
Extend the Reduction in Employees' Portion of the Payroll Tax and Extend Emergency Unemployment Benefits[d]	108	150
Implement the Policies Assumed in the Alternative Fiscal Scenario[a,e]	395	532
Implement the Policies Assumed in the Alternative Fiscal Scenario and Extend the Reduction in Employees' Portion of the Payroll Tax and Emergency Unemployment Benefits[f]	503	682

Source: Congressional Budget Office.

Notes: The estimated budgetary effects presented do not include debt service.

AMT = alternative minimum tax.

[a] The estimated effect on the budget represents the cost in fiscal years 2013 and 2014 of a 10-year extension of the policy, as shown in Congressional Budget Office, *An Update to the Budget and Economic Outlook: Fiscal Years 2012 to 2022* (August 2012).

[b] This component incorporates extensions of title I of the Tax Relief, Unemployment Insurance Reauthorization, and Job Creation Act of 2010 (which extended for 2011 and 2012 income tax provisions enacted in 2001, 2003, and 2009); of title III of that act (which modified estate and gift taxation for 2010 through 2012); of the higher exemption amount for the AMT (which was previously increased through the end of December 2011), along with an indexing of higher exemption amount and AMT tax brackets for inflation after 2011; of the treatment of nonrefundable personal credits (which also was continued through the end of 2011); and of about 80 other tax provisions (many of which expired at the end of December 2011). Nearly all of those 80 provisions have been extended previously; some, such as the research and experimentation tax credit, have been extended more than once.

[c] This component incorporates extensions of title I of the Tax Relief, Unemployment Insurance Reauthorization, and Job Creation Act of 2010 (which extended for 2011 and 2012 income tax provisions enacted in 2001, 2003, and 2009) except for the reductions to the top two tax rates on ordinary income and to the tax rates on capital gains and dividends for taxpayers filing jointly with income above $250,000 and for single filers with income above $200,000 (with both thresholds indexed for inflation since 2009); of the elimination of limits on itemized deductions and personal exemptions except for those high-income taxpayers; of title III of that act (which modified estate and gift taxation for 2010 through 2012); and of about 80 other tax provisions (many of which expired at the end of December 2011). It also incorporates indexing the AMT for inflation.

[d] The budgetary cost is for a two-year extension of the policies.

[e] Implements the first two years of the alternative fiscal scenario, combining the first three components listed in the table.

[f] Combines the first three components and the fifth component listed in the table.

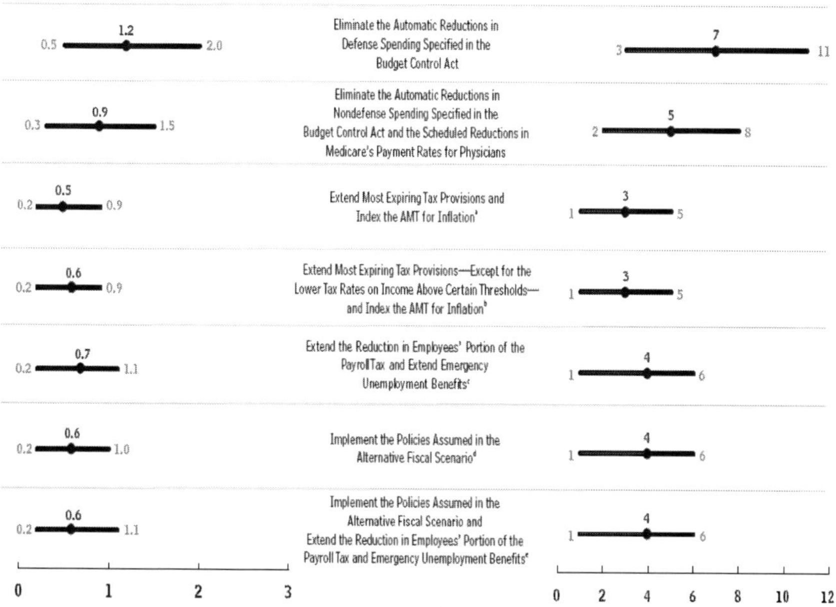

Source: Congressional Budget Office.

Notes: The estimated budgetary effects presented do not include debt service. GDP = gross domestic product; AMT = alternative minimum tax.

[a] This component incorporates extensions of title I of the Tax Relief, Unemployment Insurance Reauthorization, and Job Creation Act of 2010 (which extended for 2011 and 2012 income tax provisions enacted in 2001, 2003, and 2009); of title III of that act (which modified estate and gift taxation for 2010 through 2012); of the higher exemption amount for the AMT (which was previously increased through the end of December 2011), along with an indexing of higher exemption amount and AMT tax brackets for inflation after 2011; of the treatment of nonrefundable personal credits (which also was continued through the end of 2011); and of about 80 other tax provisions (many of which expired at the end of December 2011). Nearly all of those 80 provisions have been extended previously; some, such as the research and experimentation tax credit, have been extended more than once.

[b] This component incorporates extensions of title I of the Tax Relief, Unemployment Insurance Reauthorization, and Job Creation Act of 2010 (which extended for 2011 and 2012 income tax provisions enacted in 2001, 2003, and 2009) except for the reductions to the top two tax rates on ordinary income and to the tax rates on capital gains and dividends for taxpayers filing jointly with income above $250,000 and for single filers with income above $200,000 (with both thresholds indexed for inflation since 2009); of the elimination of limits on itemized deductions and personal exemptions except for those high-income taxpayers; of title III of that act (which modified estate and gift taxation for 2010 through 2012); and of about 80 other tax provisions (many of which expired at the end of December 2011). It also incorporates indexing the AMT for inflation.

[c] The budgetary cost is for a two-year extension of the policies.

[d] Implements the first two years of the alternative fiscal scenario, combining the first three components listed in the figure.

[e] Combines the first three components and the fifth component listed in the figure.

Figure 2. Estimated Economic Effects in 2013 of Eliminating Various Components of Fiscal Tightening Scheduled for Fiscal Years 2013 and 2014 Relative to Budgetary Costs in 2013.

Those figures represent CBO's central estimates, which correspond to the assumption that the values that describe key parameters of economic behavior (in particular, the extent to which lower federal taxes and higher federal spending boost aggregate demand in the short term) equal the midpoints of the ranges used by CBO.[11] The full ranges that CBO uses for those parameters suggest that, in the fourth quarter of 2013, real GDP could be between 0.2 percent and 0.7 percent higher, and employment 0.2 million to 0.7 million higher, if the scheduled reductions in defense outlays did not occur.

CBO measures the cost-effectiveness of a fiscal policy in generating additional output and employment by the ratio of its economic effects to its budgetary cost. On that basis, CBO estimates that eliminating the automatic reductions in defense spending would boost GDP in 2013 by about $1.20 for every dollar of budgetary cost in that year; the full range of estimates runs from $0.50 to $2.00 of GDP per dollar of budgetary cost (see Figure 2). That policy is estimated to boost employment by about 7 FTE-years in 2013 per million dollars of budgetary cost, but that amount could range from 3 to 11 FTEyears.

Eliminate the Automatic Reductions in Nondefense Spending Specified in the Budget Control Act and the Scheduled Reductions in Medicare's Payment Rates for Physicians

Estimating the amount of the automatic reductions for nondefense programs is more complicated than estimating those reductions for defense programs, particularly because provisions in the Budget Control Act limit cuts in most Medicare benefits to 2 percent and exempt many mandatory programs (including Social Security and Medicaid) from sequestration altogether. Taking those limitations into account, CBO estimated in August that, in fiscal year 2013, the automatic enforcement procedures will reduce Medicare spending by about $4 billion (including indirect effects), other mandatory spending by $5 billion, and other nondefense spending by $21 billion. In total, the enforcement procedures will reduce nondefense outlays by about $30 billion in fiscal year 2013 and by $45 billion in fiscal year 2014.

In addition, under current law, spending for Medicare will be constrained starting in January 2013 by a rate-setting system called the sustainable growth rate, which controls the fees that physicians receive for their services. If the system is allowed to operate as currently structured, physicians' fees will be reduced by 27 percent at the beginning of the year and by additional amounts in subsequent years, CBO projected in August. If, instead, lawmakers override those scheduled reductions—as they have every year since 2003—spending on Medicare would be greater than the amounts projected in CBO's baseline. For example, if payment rates stayed as they are now, outlays for Medicare (net of premiums) would be $10 billion higher in fiscal year 2013 and $16 billion higher in fiscal year 2014 than they are in CBO's current-law baseline.[12]

Together, eliminating the automatic reductions in nondefense spending and maintaining Medicare's current payment rates for physicians would increase outlays by $40 billion in fiscal year 2013 and by $61 billion in fiscal year 2014, according to CBO's estimates.

CBO projects that the additional spending would increase real GDP by 0.4 percent (by 0.1 percent to 0.6 percent under CBO's full range of assumptions) and increase full-time-equivalent employment by 0.4 million (with a range from 0.1 million to 0.7 million) in the fourth quarter of 2013. Dividing those economic effects by the budgetary cost of the policies yields an estimated increase in GDP of about $0.90 in 2013 for every dollar of budgetary cost in that year (the full range of estimates runs from $0.30 to $1.50); the increase in employment would be about 5 FTE-years in 2013 per million dollars of budgetary cost (the full range is from 2 to 8 FTEyears).

Those economic effects per dollar are smaller than the effects of the changes in defense spending because a larger share of the affected nondefense spending represents government payments to people or state and local governments, rather than direct purchases of goods and services. Because people and state and local governments would not spend all of such payments in 2013, the increases in nondefense spending have a smaller per-dollar effect on aggregate demand.

Extend Most Expiring Tax Provisions and Index the AMT for Inflation

CBO projects that federal revenues will increase by about one-third between fiscal years 2012 and 2014 as a result of several factors, including the scheduled expiration at the end of 2012 of a number of tax provisions and the expiration at the end of 2011 of certain provisions related to the AMT. As a result, under current law, revenues will reach 19.6 percent of GDP in 2014, compared with 15.8 percent in 2012, CBO estimates.

Under the rules that govern CBO's baseline, all of the provisions of the Tax Relief, Unemployment Insurance Reauthorization, and Job Creation Act of 2010 are assumed to expire as scheduled. Those expirations will increase revenues in 2013 by raising individual income tax rates, reducing the child tax credit, eliminating the American Opportunity Tax Credit, raising estate tax rates, lowering the effective exemption amount for the AMT (which rose at the end of December 2011), and making other changes.

In addition, numerous other tax provisions—beyond the income tax, estate and gift tax, and AMT provisions— expired at the end of 2011 or are scheduled to expire at

some point during the next 10 years. The staff of the Joint Committee on Taxation (JCT) and CBO estimate that the total impact of extending all expiring tax provisions (other than the cut in the payroll tax that has been in effect since the beginning of 2011) and indexing the AMT for inflation beginning in 2012 would be to reduce revenues and increase outlays for refundable tax credits by $330 billion in fiscal year 2013 and by $420 billion in fiscal year 2014. CBO estimates that such a change in law would increase real GDP by 1.4 percent (by between 0.3 percent and 2.5 percent under CBO's full range of assumptions) and increase full-time-equivalent employment by 1.8 million (with a range from 0.5 million to 3.1 million) in the fourth quarter of 2013. Dividing those economic effects by the budgetary cost of the change yields an estimated increase in GDP in 2013 of about $0.50 for every dollar of budgetary cost in that year (the full range of estimates runs from $0.20 to $0.90) and an estimated increase in employment of about 3 FTE-years in 2013 per million dollars of budgetary cost (the full range is from 1 to 5 FTE-years).[13] The estimated economic impact of those policies per dollar of budgetary cost is smaller than that of eliminating the scheduled reductions in spending because people would save some of their extra after-tax income rather than spending it all in 2013. As a result, the short-run increase in aggregate demand and output would be smaller than it would be for increased government purchases of goods and services, which would directly add dollar for dollar to aggregate demand in 2013.

Extend Most Expiring Tax Provisions—Except for the Lower Tax Rates on Income Above Certain Thresholds—and Index the AMT for Inflation

The budgetary cost of extending the expiring tax provisions would be lower if certain provisions were allowed to expire that otherwise would apply to some high-income households.[14] According to JCT and CBO's estimates, if the AMT was indexed for inflation beginning in 2012 and all of the other expiring tax provisions were extended except for the specific provisions affecting high-income taxpayers (and the payroll tax cut), revenues would be lower and outlays for refundable credits would be higher by $288 billion in fiscal year 2013 and by $382 billion in fiscal year 2014, compared with CBO's baseline projections.

CBO estimates that such changes would increase real GDP by 1.3 percent (by 0.3 percent to 2.3 percent under CBO's full range of assumptions), and increase full-time-equivalent employment by 1.6 million (with a range from 0.5 million to 2.8 million) in the fourth quarter of 2013. Dividing those economic effects by the budgetary cost yields an estimated increase in GDP of about $0.60 in 2013 for every dollar of budgetary cost in that year, with the full range of estimates running between $0.20 and $0.90, and an estimated increase in employment of about 3 FTE-years in 2013 per million dollars of budgetary cost, with a full range from 1 to 5 FTE-years.

The estimated economic effects per dollar of budgetary cost of these changes in law are slightly larger than those of extending all of the expiring tax provisions (except for the payroll tax cut) and indexing the AMT for inflation because the income affected by the higher tax rate under this policy would be that of high-income taxpayers, who, in comparison with others, probably save a larger portion and spend a smaller portion of each dollar of reduced taxes. However, the differences in the estimated effects of the two sets of policies are small (and therefore are generally not visible in the rounded numbers shown in Figure 2 on page 8), in part because the tax savings on income above the specified thresholds are a small share of the total tax savings under the broader option and in part because high-income taxpayers are presumed to save only a modestly larger portion of reductions in their taxes.

Extend the Reduction in Employees' Portion of the Payroll Tax and Extend Emergency Unemployment Benefits

Employees' share of the payroll tax was reduced by 2 percentage points (from 6.2 percent to 4.2 percent) for calendar years 2011 and 2012, reducing federal revenues in fiscal years 2011 through 2013. CBO estimates that the scheduled expiration of that tax cut will boost revenues as a share of GDP by 0.7 percentage points between 2012 and 2014.

Emergency unemployment compensation, which was extended in the Middle Class Tax Relief and Job Creation Act of 2012, is scheduled to expire at the end of 2012, so people will not be eligible to receive such benefits next year or beyond. As a result, outlays for unemployment compensation will be smaller in 2013 than in 2012 for any given level of unemployment.

If the cut in the payroll tax and eligibility to receive emergency unemployment benefits were extended through 2014, revenues would be lower and benefit payments higher by a combined $108 billion in fiscal year 2013 and $150 billion in fiscal year 2014.[15] Those changes in law would increase real GDP by 0.7 percent (by 0.2 percent to 1.2 percent under CBO's full range of assumptions) and increase full-time-equivalent employment by 0.8 million (with a range from 0.3 million to 1.3 million) in the fourth quarter of 2013, CBO estimates. Dividing those economic effects by the budgetary cost yields an estimated increase in GDP of about $0.70 in 2013 for every dollar of budgetary cost in that year, with the full range of estimates running from $0.20 and $1.10, and an increase in employment of about 4 FTE-years in 2013 per million dollars of budgetary cost, with a full range from 1 to 6 FTE-years.

The estimated economic impact of those policies per dollar of budgetary cost is larger than that of extending other expiring tax provisions and indexing the AMT for inflation because a larger share of the additional unemployment benefits and extended payroll tax cut would be spent by the recipients in 2013. As a result, the short-run increase in aggregate demand and output would be greater.

Implement All of the Policies Assumed in the Alternative Fiscal Scenario

Making all of the changes included in the first two years of CBO's alternative fiscal scenario—namely, making all of the changes to federal spending described above, extending all of the expiring tax provisions (except the payroll tax cut), and indexing the AMT for inflation— would increase spending and reduce taxes by a combined $395 billion in fiscal year 2013 and $532 billion in 2014 (excluding the effects on interest payments), according to JCT and CBO's estimates in August.

CBO estimates that such changes in law would boost real GDP by 2.2 percent (by between 0.6 percent and 3.9 percent under CBO's full range of assumptions) and increase full-time-equivalent employment by 2.7 million (with a range from 0.8 million to 4.5 million) in the fourth quarter of 2013. About two-thirds of those effects would owe to changes in tax policies and about one-third to changes in spending policies. The economic effects of the tax and spending changes are not proportional to their budgetary effects because, by CBO's estimates, the spending changes would boost GDP more than the tax changes would for each dollar of budgetary cost.

Implement All of the Policies Assumed in the Alternative Fiscal Scenario and Extend the Payroll Tax Reduction and Emergency Unemployment Benefits

Making all of the changes included in the first two years of CBO's alternative fiscal scenario as well as extending both the reduction in the payroll tax and emergency unemployment benefits would increase the deficit by $503 billion in 2013 and by $682 billion in 2014. CBO estimates that such changes in law would boost real GDP by 2.9 percent (by between 0.8 percent and 5.0 percent under CBO's full range of assumptions) and increase full-time-equivalent employment by 3.4 million (with a range from 1.1 million to 5.8 million) in the fourth quarter of 2013.[16]

CBO's August 2012 projection of the deficit under current law in fiscal year 2013—$641 billion—would represent a decline in the deficit of $448 billion from fiscal year 2012 to fiscal year 2013; that amount is less than the estimated $503 billion budgetary cost in 2013 of the combination of the policies in the alternative fiscal scenario plus extension of the payroll tax cut and emergency unemployment benefits.[17] That difference occurs because CBO's baseline projection of the deficit includes effects on the budget of the macroeconomic impact of the scheduled fiscal tightening, other scheduled changes in policy not part of the combination being analyzed here, and other factors that normally affect year-to-year changes in revenues and spending.

Longer-Term Effects of Policies Contributing to Fiscal Tightening

Although reducing the fiscal tightening scheduled to occur next year would boost output and employment in the short run, doing so without imposing a comparable amount of additional tightening in future years would reduce the nation's output and income in the longer run relative to what would occur if the scheduled tightening remained in place. If all of the policies considered in this analysis were extended for a prolonged period beyond the two years assumed here, federal debt held by the public— which is currently more than 70 percent of GDP, its highest mark since 1950—would continue to rise much faster than GDP. Such a path for federal debt could not be sustained indefinitely, so policy changes would be required at some point.[18]

Over the longer term, the nation's potential to produce goods and services is the key determinant of output and income. That potential depends on the size and quality of the labor force, the stock of productive capital (such as factories, vehicles, and computers), and the efficiency with which labor and capital are used. Lasting changes in those factors can have an enduring influence on the economy's ability to produce goods and services.

Federal budget policies affect potential output mainly by affecting the amount of public saving (the combined surpluses or deficits run by the federal government and state and local governments) and the incentives for people and businesses to work, save, and invest. Different methods of achieving any given increase in public saving could have different effects on those incentives. For example, increases in marginal tax rates on labor would tend to reduce the amount of labor supplied to the economy, whereas increases in revenues of a similar magnitude from broadening the tax base would probably have a smaller negative impact or even a positive impact on the supply of labor.[19] Similarly, cutting government benefit payments would generally strengthen people's incentive to work and save, but the actual impact would depend on the nature of the cuts.

CBO has not estimated the longer-term economic effects of the fiscal policies analyzed in this report, but the agency has estimated the effect on output that would occur in 2022 under the alternative fiscal scenario, which incorporates the assumption that several of the policies are maintained indefinitely. CBO estimates that in 2022, on net, the policies included in the alternative fiscal scenario would reduce real GDP by 0.4 percent and real gross national product (GNP) by 1.7 percent.[20] That projected effect primarily reflects two opposing forces: People's incentives to work and save would be greater with that scenario's lower tax rates, but the larger budget deficits and rapidly growing federal debt would hamper national saving and investment and thus reduce output and income.

In years beyond 2022, rising deficits under the alternative fiscal scenario would lead to larger negative effects on GDP and GNP and to larger increases in interest rates relative to the rates that would prevail under current law. Ultimately, the policies assumed in the alternative fiscal scenario would lead to unsustainable federal debt, from both an economic and a budgetary perspective.

End Notes

[1] The figures in this paragraph are unchanged from those in CBO's previous analysis of this issue. See Congressional Budget Office, *An Update to the Budget and Economic Outlook: Fiscal Years 2012 to 2022* (August 2012).

[2] The economic measures presented in this report apply to calendar years. The budget figures are for fiscal years, which run from October 1 through September 30.

[3] For a detailed explanation of the policies underlying the alternative fiscal scenario, see Congressional Budget Office, *An Update to the Budget and Economic Outlook: Fiscal Years 2012 to 2022* (August 2012).

[4] For additional discussion of those criteria, see the statement of Douglas W. Elmendorf, Director, Congressional Budget Office, before the Joint Select Committee on Deficit Reduction, *Confronting the Nation's Fiscal Policy Challenges* (September 13, 2011).

[5] See Congressional Budget Office, *Estimated Impact of the American Recovery and Reinvestment Act on Employment and Economic Output from April 2012 Through June 2012* (August 2012); the statement of Douglas W. Elmendorf, Director, Congressional Budget Office, before the Senate Committee on the Budget, *Policies for Increasing Economic Growth and Employment in 2012 and 2013* (November 15, 2011); and Felix Reichling and Charles Whalen, *Assessing the Short-Term Effects on Output of Changes in Federal Fiscal Policies*, Congressional Budget Office Working Paper 2012-08 (May 2012).

[6] See Nicholas Bloom, "The Impact of Uncertainty Shocks," *Econometrica*, vol. 77, no. 3 (May 2009), pp. 623–685.

[7] One might attempt to calculate the budgetary cost per FTE-year for different policies by inverting the number of cumulative years of full-time employment per million dollars of budgetary cost (reported below). However, such calculations could be misleading for two reasons. First, for many of the options considered here, employment is affected beyond 2013—in part because effects on employment tend to lag behind those on GDP. Second, CBO's ranges of estimated effects on GDP (and thereby employment) are chosen to be centered relative to the distribution of possible outcomes, but the inverses of those ranges are not necessarily centered relative to the distribution of the inverses of those outcomes.

[8] Discretionary spending is spending out of budget authority provided in appropriation acts. Mandatory spending is spending on programs that are not normally controlled by the annual appropriation process; many of them provide benefits based on formulas and eligibility criteria set in law.

[9] Budgetary resources consist of all sources of authority provided to federal agencies that permit them to incur financial obligations, including new budget authority, unobligated balances, direct spending authority, and obligation limitations.

[10] See *OMB Report Pursuant to the Sequestration Transparency Act of 2012* (September 14, 2012) for the Office of Management and Budget's estimates of the effects of the potential sequestration for 2013. Those estimates differ slightly from the totals that CBO published in August in *An Update to the Budget and Economic Outlook: Fiscal Years 2012 to 2022*.

[11] For a discussion of CBO's approach to analyzing the short-term effects of fiscal policy, see Reichling and Whalen, *Assessing the Short-Term Effects on Output of Changes in Federal Fiscal Policies*.

[12] On November 1, 2012, the Centers for Medicare and Medicaid Services issued a final rule specifying that Medicare's payment rates for physicians' services during calendar year 2013 will be 26.5 percent lower than current payment rates. That recent action is not reflected in CBO's estimates used for this report.

[13] The estimated effects on GDP per dollar of budgetary cost are somewhat larger than those CBO estimated for a similar policy in November 2011. The difference arises because the previous analysis applied to a one-year extension of expiring tax provisions and reported economic effects for that year relative to the full budgetary cost (including the part of the cost that would spill over to a second year), whereas the current analysis applies to a two-year extension of expiring tax provisions and reports economic effects for the first year relative to the budgetary cost in that year alone.

[14] Specifically, this alternative policy incorporates extensions of title I of the Tax Relief, Unemployment Insurance Reauthorization, and Job Creation Act of 2010 (which extended for 2011 and 2012 income tax provisions enacted in 2001, 2003, and 2009) except for the reductions to the top two tax rates on ordinary income and to the tax rates on capital gains and dividends for taxpayers filing jointly with income above $250,000 and for single filers with income above $200,000 (with both thresholds indexed for inflation since 2009); of the elimination of limits on itemized deductions and personal exemptions except for those high-income taxpayers; and of title III of that act (which modified estate and gift taxation for 2010 through 2012). It also incorporates indexing the AMT for inflation.

[15] The great majority of that budgetary impact—$86 billion in fiscal year 2013 and $119 billion in fiscal year 2014—stems from the payroll tax reduction. There would also be a small budgetary effect in fiscal year 2015.

[16] CBO's central estimate of a 2.9 percent increase in GDP in the fourth quarter of 2013 from the policies of the alternative fiscal scenario and extension of the payroll tax reduction and emergency unemployment benefits—undoing nearly all of the changes in policy that lead to fiscal tightening under current law—is notably smaller than a previous estimate of 3.9 percent for removing all of the scheduled fiscal restraint (see Congressional Budget Office, *Economic Effects of Reducing the Fiscal Restraint That Is Scheduled to Occur in 2013*, May 2012). Those estimates differ primarily because CBO now projects a smaller decline in the deficit between 2012 and 2013, in part because the deficit in 2012 turned out to be smaller than the agency projected.

[17] In August, CBO projected that the decline in the deficit under current law would be $487 billion. Because the deficit in 2012 turned out to be smaller than CBO projected, that difference is now $448 billion.

[18] See Congressional Budget Office, *The 2012 Long-Term Budget Outlook* (June 2012).

[19] Broadening the tax base would have opposing effects on the supply of labor. On the one hand, reducing taxpayers' after-tax income would tend to cause them to work more to make up for the loss in income. On the other hand, some approaches for broadening the base would raise some taxpayers' marginal tax rates—by pushing them into higher tax brackets, for example— which would tend to cause them to work less. Whether the net effect was positive or negative would depend upon the details of the base-broadening policy.

[20] Those figures represent CBO's central estimates, which correspond to the assumption that the values that describe key parameters of economic behavior (in particular, the extent to which higher deficits crowd out private investment and the extent to which lower marginal tax rates on labor income boost the labor supply) equal the midpoints of the ranges used by CBO. The full ranges that CBO uses for those parameters suggest that in 2022 real GDP could be between 2.0 percent lower and 2.1 percent higher, and real GNP between 3.5 percent lower and 0.9 percent higher, under the policies of the alternative fiscal scenario than under current law.

GNP differs from GDP primarily by including the capital income that residents earn from investments abroad and excluding the capital income that nonresidents earn from domestic investments. GNP is a better measure for analyzing the impact of growing deficits and debt on income because projected budget deficits would be partly financed by inflows of capital from other countries that would lead to a future flow of income to those countries.

For a more detailed discussion of CBO's longer-term estimates of economic effects of fiscal policies, see Congressional Budget Office, *The 2012 Long-Term Budget Outlook* (June 2012), pp. 29–40.

INDEX

A

B

C

D

E

F

G

H

I

P

R

S

T

U

V

W

Y